International Investment Law and Arbitration

International Investment Law and Arbitration

Editors-in-Chief

Ian A. Laird (*Crowell & Moring; Columbia Law School; Georgetown University Law Center; International Law Institute*)
Borzu Sabahi (*Curtis, Mallet-Prevost, Colt & Mosle LLP; Georgetown University Law Center; International Law Institute*)

Managing Editor

Giovanna E. Gismondi (*Managing Director, International Investment Law Center – Georgetown University*)

Advisory Board

Brooks W. Daly (*Permanent Court of Arbitration*) – Rudolf Dolzer (*University of Bonn*) – Mark Kantor (*Independent arbitrator; Georgetown University*) – Joongi Kim (*Yonsei Law School*) – Hege Elisabeth Kjos (*University of Amsterdam*) – Andrea Menaker (*White & Case LLP*) – Antonio R. Parra (*The World Bank*) – Frédéric G. Sourgens (*Washburn University School of Law*) – Sylvie Tabet (*Trade Law Bureau, Government of Canada*) – Todd Weiler (*Independent counsel, consultant, expert, and arbritrator*) – Anne Marie Whitesell (*Professor, Georgetown University Law Center*)

Associate Editors

Paul Barker (*Barrister, Doughty Street Chambers, London*) – Nicholas J. Birch (*Stewart and Stewart*) – Kabir Duggal (*Senior Associate, Baker & McKenzie LLP; Lecturer-in-Law, Columbia Law School*) – John Laird (*Crowell & Moring*) – Diora M. Ziyaeva (*Dentons LLP*)

Volumes published in this Brill Research Perspectives title are listed at *brill.com/rpia*

International Investment Law and Arbitration

History, Modern Practice, and Future Prospects

By

Borzu Sabahi
Ian A. Laird
Giovanna E. Gismondi

BRILL

LEIDEN | BOSTON

This paperback book edition is simultaneously published as issue 1.1 (2017) of *International Investment Law and Arbitration*, DOI 10.1163/24055778-12340001.

Library of Congress Control Number: 2017963454

Typeface for the Latin, Greek, and Cyrillic scripts: "Brill". See and download: brill.com/brill-typeface.

ISBN 978-90-04-36302-1 (paperback)
ISBN 978-90-04-36303-8 (e-book)

Copyright 2018 by Borzu Sabahi, Ian A. Laird, and Giovanna E. Gismondi.
Published by Koninklijke Brill NV, Leiden, The Netherlands.
Koninklijke Brill NV incorporates the imprints Brill, Brill Hes & De Graaf, Brill Nijhoff, Brill Rodopi, Brill Sense and Hotei Publishing.
Koninklijke Brill NV reserves the right to protect the publication against unauthorized use and to authorize dissemination by means of offprints, legitimate photocopies, microform editions, reprints, translations, and secondary information sources, such as abstracting and indexing services including databases. Requests for commercial re-use, use of parts of the publication, and/or translations must be addressed to Koninklijke Brill NV.

This book is printed on acid-free paper and produced in a sustainable manner.

Contents

International Investment Law and Arbitration: History, Modern Practice, and Future Prospects 1
 Borzu Sabahi, Ian A. Laird, and Giovanna E. Gismondi
 Abstract 1
 Keywords 2
 I. Introduction 2
 II. Forces that Shape the System of Investment Protection and Promotion 3
  A. *Ideologies, Political Economy, and the Historical Context* 3
  B. *Protagonists* 4
  C. *The Nature of the Modern System of Investor-State Arbitration* 5
 III. Genesis of the Law: Protection of Aliens Abroad, Gunboat Diplomacy, Minimum Standard, and Diplomatic Protection 7
 IV. Protection through Peaceful Means of Settlement of Disputes: Hague Conferences, PCIJ, ICJ 11
 V. Post-World War II: Promotion and Protection of Private Capital Flows 13
  A. *Security for Foreign Investment through Investment Guarantees* 13
  B. *Security through Arbitration: Creation of the World Bank's International Centre for Settlement of Investment Disputes* 15
  C. *Contractual Techniques to Protect Foreign Investment* 16
  D. *The New International Economic Order (NIEO)* 17
 VI. FCN and BIT Programs and Recognition of Foreign Investor's Right to Directly Submit Claims to International Arbitration without Espousal or Exhaustion of Local Remedies 19
  A. *Overview* 19
  B. *Post-Cold War: Proliferation of BITs and Investment Treaty Disputes* 20
  C. *First Test of the Investment Treaty System: Early NAFTA and the Argentine Financial Crisis Cases* 21
 VII. Content of Modern BITs 23
  A. *Investor's Right to Directly Initiate Arbitration and the Idea of Unilateral Consent* 24
  B. *Admission and Establishment* 25
  C. *Key Substantive Protections for Foreign Investors* 27
  D. *Key Aspects of the Investor State-Arbitration Process* 31

VIII. Scaling Back Protections and Backlash   44
    A.   *The EU Proposal of a European Investment Court System*   44
    B.   *The US Proposal for a Revised NAFTA*   49
IX. Conclusion   52

Bibliography   53

International Investment Law and Arbitration: History, Modern Practice, and Future Prospects

Borzu Sabahi
Georgetown University Law Center
bsabahi@curtis.com

Ian A. Laird
Georgetown University Law Center
Ilaird@crowell.com

Giovanna E. Gismondi
Georgetown University Law Center
geg33@georgetown.edu

Abstract

International Investment Law is one of the most dynamically growing fields of International Law as shown by the volume of Bilateral Investment Treaties (BITs), and investment chapters in a growing numbers of regional and mega-regional trade agreements. This paper explores the origin, evolution and operation of International Investment Law. It discusses the main actors, the protections afforded to foreign investments and investors, and the content of modern BITs. The legal issues and challenges International Investment Law faces today are brought into perspective. Particularly, this paper provides an assessment of the measures put forth by the European Union aimed at transforming the traditional investor-State arbitration system to an Investment Court System. An examination of the NAFTA re-negotiations is also presented, including the impact that CETA, a trade deal between the EU and Canada could have in the outcome of the current re-negotiations.

---

* The authors acknowledge research assistance of Saud Aldawsari. All errors remain ours and the views expressed here solely those of the authors and cannot be attributed to Crowell & Moring LLP and Curtis Mallet-Prevost Colt & Mosle LLP.

Keywords

History of International Investment Law – Mixed Claims Commissions – Diplomatic Protection – Espousal – Bilateral Investment Treaties (BITS) – Investor-State Dispute Settlement Mechanism – Investment Court System (ICS) – NAFTA

I   Introduction

Welcome to the Brill Research Perspectives on International Investment Law and Arbitration. This new series aims to provide a new approach to the coverage of the modern international law on foreign investment. This field of public international law has a unique overlap with topics found in private international law, international dispute resolution, as well as national laws. International investment law is predominantly made up of a vast network of more than 3000 bilateral investment treaties and free trade agreements, with their unique direct right of investor-State arbitration[1] for foreign investors, together with host State laws regulating foreign investment, investment contracts, and political risk insurance schemes.

To fully understand how this system was created, how it is functioning and how it is evolving, little would be achieved if one were to only analyze those sources. Behind the black letter law is a host of persons and entities, which are in pursuit of specific objectives in this living system and would influence the law and the law-making process to achieve those objectives. This veritable group shapes what we think of as a system of international investment law, norms and values.[2] An assessment of the system, therefore, should take contribution of all these groups into account so as to provide a full picture of this important regime.

In this context, the question of what exactly is investment law in contrast to policy, and how the two interact with each other, while an important exercise on its own, is something that perhaps should be best left for experts in Positivism and the New Haven school to debate.[3] Our objective is more

---

1   Also referred to as "investor-State dispute settlement" or "ISDS."
2   Although some have questioned whether this is in fact a system. *See* discussion *infra* Part II.C.
3   For a concise overview of New Heaven school *see* W. Michael Reisman, *The View from the New Haven School of International Law*, AMERICAN SOCIETY OF INTERNATIONAL LAW, PROCEEDINGS OF THE ANNUAL MEETING 118, 120 (1992) (comparing the jurisprudential

modest for this new series, and more pragmatic in that we envision for this first Issue of the Brill Research Perspectives on International Investment Law and Arbitration to serve as a roadmap for the readers and contributors on important topics that the series will seek to cover. The identification of various issues here of course is not exhaustive and, with time and new developments, new issues may arise which may be covered in the series.

II   Forces that Shape the System of Investment Protection and Promotion

A   *Ideologies, Political Economy, and the Historical Context*

The law over the course of history has been employed to implement economic policy or the prevailing economic theories of the day.[4] The modern system for the protection of foreign investment, particularly bilateral investment treaties ('BITS'), is not an exception and seems to have been heavily influenced by the economic liberalism ideologies perfected in the Eighteenth Century by Adam Smith and others.[5] Those ideas are the spine of the modern market economies, and promote a spectrum of policies ranging from freedom of movement of capital, to respect for private property rights and contracts.[6]

Investment treaties, particularly after the collapse of the Soviet Union, became popular under the perception that they would contribute to the attraction of foreign direct investment,[7] leading to the conclusion of 3,079 BITS between 1990 and 2015.[8] Modern investment treaties, particularly BITS, adopt

---

and intellectual approaches of Positivism and the New Haven school). On Positivism see John Gardner, *Legal Positivism: 5 ½ Myths*, 46 AM J. OF JURIS. 199 (2001).

4   *See generally* Ejan Mackaay, *History of Law and Economics*, *in* 1 ENCYCLOPEDIA OF LAW AND ECONOMICS 65 (Boudewijn Bouckaert & Gerrit De Geest eds., 2000).

5   Kenneth J. Vandevelde, *The Political Economy of a Bilateral Investment Treaty*, 92 AM. J. INT'L L. 621, 623 ("Liberal economic theorists, particularly Adam Smith and David Ricardo, sought to demonstrate that free markets, unfettered by state regulation, would result in the greatest prosperity for all.... [Economic] Liberalism also has advocated the free movement of capital across borders."); *see also* M. SORNARAJAH, RESISTANCE AND CHANGE IN THE INTERNATIONAL LAW OF FOREIGN INVESTMENT 269 (2015).

6   *See* E. WAYNE NAFZIGER, THE ECONOMICS OF DEVELOPING COUNTRIES 110–13 (3rd ed. 1997); *see also* Vandevelde, *supra* note 5, at 624; SORNARAJAH, *supra* note 5, at 296.

7   *See infra* Part VI.B (discussing the uncertainty of the effects of BITS on FDIS).

8   INVESTMENT POLICY HUB, http://investmentpolicyhub.unctad.org/ (last visited Sept. 30, 2015).

to a large degree those ideals in various provisions, which protect and promote private capital flows, especially in their preambles where they recognize for example "that [the] agreement ... will stimulate the flow of private capital and the economic development of the Parties".[9]

B   Protagonists

It has been suggested that the positive law should be policy neutral. In other words, once States transform their intentions into treaty terms, those terms would then take a life of their own and would be immune from manipulation by external forces.[10] Human ingenuity, however, seems to defy this mantra.[11] In modern international investment law, a variety of interested persons who influence the system and the rules of the game, are involved.[12] We call them 'the protagonists'. The list is long and includes: States which negotiated the treaties, bringing their bargaining powers and their geopolitical status in

---

[9] Treaty between the Government of the United States of America and the Government of [Country] Concerning the Encouragement and Reciprocal Protection Investment [hereinafter US Model BIT 2012].

[10] Under the classical theory of positivism, international lawyers are to interpret the law objectively because the authentic wills of the states are stated in these rules. Hence "[t]his system of rules is an 'objective' reality and needs to be distinguished from law 'as it should be.'" Bruno Simma & Andreas L. Paulus, *Symposium on Method in International Law: The Responsibility of Individuals for Human Rights Abuses in Internal Conflicts: A Positivist View*, 93 AM. J. INT'L L. 302, 304 (1999). Viewed differently, the central claim is that "[i]n any legal system, whether a given norm is legally valid, and hence whether it forms part of the law of that system, depends on its sources, not its merits." Gardner, *supra* note 3. Positivism, therefore, mandates strict separation between the laws in force that are derived from a unified system of law from non-legal factors such as political ideologies, moral judgments, natural laws. Id.; *see also* Tai-Heng Cheng, *Positivism, New Haven Jurisprudence, and the Fragmentation of International Law*, *in* NEW DIRECTIONS IN INTERNATIONAL ECONOMIC LAW 411 (Todd Weiler & Freya Baetens eds., 2011) (discussing the New Haven views and Positivists views as thinking frameworks for modern legal systems).

[11] Sornarajah even goes so far as to suggest the system of Positivism was intentionally used to disguise the true intentions behind the idea of the law's neutrality. SORNARAJAH, *supra* note 5, at 20 ("The positivist view of moral and political neutrality has often been the means of hiding the interests of powers and the fact that power shapes the law. It enables the cloaking of power relationships that affect the formation of rules by ensuring that there was no need for inquiry into factors that are extraneous to the law and legal rules in studying the formation and function of the law.").

[12] Anthea Roberts, *Clash of Paradigms: Actors and Analogies Shaping the Investment Treaty System*, 107 AM. J. INT'L L. 45, 53 (2013) (analyzing the different actors that influence the system).

the global economic and power structure; individuals and corporations which are the primary beneficiaries of investment treaties; various non-governmental organizations and interest groups; institutions that administer arbitral proceedings; inter-governmental institutions involved in research and development work; and counsel, experts, scholars and arbitrators who apply the law and comment upon it.[13] A full understanding of the system of international investment law would require an assessment of the protagonists' views and objectives.

C   *The Nature of the Modern System of Investor-State Arbitration*

In recent years, several commentators have attempted to propose comprehensive theories to rationalize the modern system of international investment law, presumably to introduce some measure of clarity and consistency.[14] Dolzer and Schreuer, for example, are of the view that it is only a matter of semantics to speak of the existence of a separate category of principles of international investment law given their strong link to international economic law in general. However, the nature, structure, and purpose of international investment law stands out as structurally different in the broader international picture.[15] Zachary Douglas considers the system as a "hybrid" one due to the fact that public international law and domestic law both play a role and interact.[16] Benedict Kingsbury and Stephan Schill consider it as part of an emerging global administrative law.[17] Santiago Montt perceives it as a species of global

---

13   Id.
14   Joost Pauwlyn has argued that the modern investor-State arbitration system does not create a regime in international law. Joost Pauwelyn, *At the Edge of Chaos? Foreign Investment Law as a Complex Adaptive System, How It Emerged and How It Can Be Reformed*, 29 ICSID REV. 372, 372 (2014) (citation omitted) ("Second, how can [Foreign Investment Law] survive, let alone constitute a 'system' or 'regime', given its composition of thousands of treaties, custom, domestic laws, contracts and (often contradictory) arbitration awards, without a controlling multilateral treaty or institution, or appellate court?"). *Cf.* Jose Alvarez points to the substantial degree of legalization of international investment flows. "Like many other international regimes, this 'move to law' has proceeded along three dimensions: increasing levels of obligation, precision, and delegation". Jose Enrique Alvarez, The Public International Law Regime Governing International Investment, 344 Collected Courses of the Hague Academy of International Law 193, 211 (2009).
15   Rudolf Dolzer & Christoph Schreuer, Principles of International Investment Law 74–75 (2nd ed., 2012).
16   Zachary Douglas, *The Hybrid Foundations of Investment Treaty Arbitration*, 74 BRIT. Y.B. INT'L L. 151, 151–55 (2003).
17   Benedict Kingsbury & Stephan Schill, Investor-State Arbitration as Governance: Fair and Equitable Treatment, Proportionality and the Emerging Global Administrative Law, 1–8

administrative law.[18] Gus van Harten considers the system as species of public law.[19] Thomas Wälde emphasized the State-individual paradigm, which underscores every modern investment treaty case, and suggested that to understand and further develop this system one must draw analogies with those areas of law where similar paradigms exist.[20] He ultimately saw the system as an external discipline and a vehicle for promoting good governance.[21] Stephan Schill, focusing on the role of most favored nation clauses, posits that bilateral investment treaties ultimately contribute to the creation of a single and comprehensive multilateral investment system.[22]

Anthea Roberts describes the abstruse nature of the regime in the following anecdote:

> When the skin of an Australian platypus was first taken to England in the 1700s, scientists thought it was a fake. It looked like someone had sewn a duck's bill onto a beaver's body; one scientist even took a pair of scissors to the skin looking for stitches. The animal had fur and was warm-blooded like a mammal, yet laid eggs and had webbed feet like a bird or a reptile. Scientists struggled to categorize this unusual creature. Was

(September 2, 2009), NYU School of Law, Public Law Research Paper No. 09-46, *available at* http://ssrn.com/abstract=1466980.

18   SANTIAGO MONTT, STATE LIABILITY IN INVESTMENT TREATY ARBITRATION: GLOBAL CONSTITUTIONAL LAW AND ADMINISTRATIVE LAW IN THE BIT GENERATION (2009).

19   Gus Van Harten, *The Public-Private Distinction in the International Arbitration of Individual Claims Against the State*, 56 International & Comparative Law Quarterly (ICLQ) 371–73 (2007).

20   Philip Kahn and Thomas Wälde, Report for the Hague Academy 2004 in connection with the program "New Aspects of International Investment Law / Les aspects nouveaux du droit des investissements internationaux" (Ph. Kahn and T. W. Wälde eds., 2004).

21   Thomas Wälde, *Investment Arbitration as a Discipline for Good Governance*: Overview and Epilogue, [Oil, Gas & Energy Law], issue 2, 2004, at 1, 17; see also Nicholas J. Birch, Ian Laird, Borzu Sabahi, International Investment Law Regime and the Rule of Law as a Precondition for International Development, *in* NEW DIRECTIONS IN INTERNATIONAL ECONOMIC LAW (Todd Weiler & Freya Baetens eds., 2011).

22   STEPHAN W. SCHILL, THE MULTILATERALIZATION OF INTERNATIONAL INVESTMENT LAW 15–16 (Cambridge University Press 2009) ("the consistent failure of multilateral instruments and the rise of bilateral treaties do not imply that multilateralism as an institution in investment relations has not materialized to a certain extent.... BITs in their entirety ... function analogously to a truly multilateral system as they establish rather uniform general principles that order the relations between foreign investors and host States in a relatively uniform manner independently of the sources and targets of specific transborder investment flows").

it a bird, a mammal, or a reptile? Or was it some strange hybrid of all three? Comprehending the investment treaty system has proven just as problematic.[23]

Anthea Roberts endorses the "system's sui generis nature, which will likely draw on insights from multiple paradigms instead of endorsing any single one."[24]

III   Genesis of the Law: Protection of Aliens Abroad, Gunboat Diplomacy, Minimum Standard, and Diplomatic Protection

The lineage of the law on *protection* (vis-à-vis promotion) of foreign investment goes back to measures that various States took to protect the person and property of their nationals abroad.[25] During the 19th and early 20th century (and even during earlier periods) foreign nationals or aliens who lived in foreign lands often had little redress if they suffered injustice.[26] In that period, courts or other authorities for seeking redress may not have existed, or provided sufficient protection, or may even have been biased towards local interests.[27]

---

23   Anthea Roberts, *supra* note 12, at 46.
24   Id. at 94.
25   Hans W. Spiegel, *Origin and Development of Denial of Justice*, 32 Am. J. Int'l L. 63 (1938); Chittharanjan Felix Amerasinghe, Local Remedies in International Law 25 (2nd ed. 2004) (discussing the historical roots of alien protection); Kate Parlett, The Individual in the International Legal System: Continuity and Change in International Law 50 (2011).
26   Christopher Dugan, Don Wallace, Noah Rubins & Borzu Sabahi, Investor-State Arbitration 13 (2008) [hereinafter Dugan et al.] (discussing barriers to recovery by foreign investors).
27   *See* id. Local bias is an old and common phenomenon everywhere including in most developed countries. The *Loewen* case is a modern example. *Loewen Group, Inc. v. United States of America*, ICSID Case No. ARB(AF)/98/3, Award, ¶ 35 (June 26, 2003). The Loewen's claim arose from a 1995 verdict rendered by a Mississippi state court against the Canadian claimant and in favor of an American competitor, Mr. O'Keefe. Id. ¶ 3. The jury awarded O'Keefe $500 million damages, including $75 million damages for emotional distress and $400 million punitive damages in a US$4 million breach of contract case. The judge repeatedly allowed O'Keefe's flamboyant attorney to make irrelevant and prejudicial references, anti-Canadian comments, racial slurs, and class biases. Id. ¶ 59. Loewen unable to post an appeal bond equal to 125% of the verdict had to forego the appeal and ultimately agreed to pay $175 million as settlement.

The European powers[28] as well as the United States,[29] therefore, frequently used so-called "gunboat diplomacy" by which home states of the investor would rely on the threat of superior force or economic sanctions to protect the interests of their nationals. In addition, these nations, particularly the United States, took the initiative to develop legal doctrines giving rise to the creation

---

28   The Don Pacifico affair is an episode of gunboat diplomacy that concerned the United Kingdom, Greece, and Portugal. Pacifico, a British citizen residing in Athens, was the subject of mob violence in April 1847. His attackers were even aided by the police. Pacifico alleged £30,000 in damages, which he tried to recover from the Government of Greece to no avail. After failed diplomatic communications the British Government instituted a pacific blockade on the coast of Greece. This brought protests from the French and the Russians, with whom Britain shared a protectorate of Greece. Ultimately, the issue was arbitrated and Pacifico was able to recover from the government of Portugal and later from the Greek Government which paid two third of his original claim. The incident had a significant impact on the internal politics of Britain. In a famous five-hour speech to the House of Commons, Lord Palmerston, Britain's foreign secretary, defended the policy. He made comparison between the British empire and the Roman empire; that "just as a Roman could claim his rights anywhere in the world with the words 'Civis Romanus sum' ('I am a Roman citizen'), 'so also a British subject, in whatever land he may be, shall feel confident that the watchful eye and the strong arm of England will protect him against injustice and wrong.'" *Don Pacifico Affair*, ENCYCLOPÆDIA BRITANNICA, http://www.britannica.com/event/Don-Pacifico-affair (last visited Oct. 2, 2015); Goebel, Julius Jr., *The International Responsibility of States for Injuries Sustained by Aliens on Account of Mob Violence, Insurrections and Civil Wars*, 8 AM. J. INT'L L. 802, 820 (1914). Another example is the Venezualan blockade crises. The blockade was imposed by Britain, Germany, and Italy over Venezuela for refusal to pay damages sustained by European citizens during the civil war. NANCY MITCHELL, THE DANGER OF DREAMS: GERMAN AND AMERICAN IMPERIALISM IN LATIN AMERICA 62 (1999).

29   The United States in several occasions sent out gunboats particularly to collect debt from various Latin American nations. Indeed, the Drago Doctrine was a reaction to the gunboat diplomacy to collect debt in Latin America and the military pressures of the Venezuelan blockade crisis. The doctrine was the creation of the Argentinian international lawyer Luis Maria Drago as a response to political and military pressure from Great Britain, Germany, and Italy against Venezuela. Drago sent a letter to the Minster of the Argentine republic condemning the use of gunboat diplomacy to collect a public debt from a sovereign American state by the use of armed force. *See* Kathryn Sikkink, *Reconceptualizing Sovereignty in the Americas: Historical Precursors and Current Practices*, 19 HOUS. J. INT'L L. 705, 716 (1997); Denise Manning-Cabrol, *The Imminent Death of the Calvo Clause and the Rebirth of the Calvo Principle: Equality of Foreign and National Investors*, 26 LAW & POL'Y INT'L BUS. 1169, 1174 & n. 25–26 (1995); Yessika Monagas, *U.S. Property in Jeopardy: Latin American Expropriations of U.S. Corporations' Property Abroad*, 34 HOUS. J. INT'L L. 455, 489–90 (2012).

of a body of law known broadly as the law on protection of aliens.[30] Among other components, the US developed the idea of a minimum standard for protection of aliens in international law.[31] The standard mandated that disputes between foreign investors and host states should be settled by extraterritorial neutral tribunals in accordance with international legal principles that were built into the rules of diplomatic protection of nationals abroad.[32] Included in that law was the idea that expropriation of aliens' property had to be accompanied by compensation.[33] The US Secretary of State, Cordell Hull, in 1938 described this idea as: "*the right* of prompt and just compensation for expropriated property....".[34] This statement solidified the American position.

Latin American States, which were the recipients of substantial American investment, rejected the American approach. To counter the minimum standard theory, the Argentine jurist, Carlos Calvo, devised in the mid-19th century what later became known as the *Calvo doctrine*. Under the doctrine, a host Government did not have to grant treatment any more favorable than that granted to its own nationals.[35] The Mexican Minister of Foreign

---

30   EDWIN BORCHARD, THE DIPLOMATIC PROTECTION OF CITIZENS ABROAD (1915).

31   The United States played a more active role here than the European powers for the simple reason that on the European side, most problems arose in the context of handling relationships with colonies whereas the United States, particularly from the early to mid-Nineteenth century had to deal with already independent Latin American nations requiring a more nuanced approach. *See* SORNARAJAH, *supra* note 5, at 32. On the minimum standard see Frederick S. Dunn, The protection of nationals: a study in the application of international law (1932); Andreas H. Roth, The minimum standard of international law applied to aliens (1949); Edwin Borchard, *Minimum Standard of Treatment of Aliens*, 33 ASIL Proc. 51 (1939). See also reports of the U.N. Special Rapporteur John Dugard on diplomatic protection, *available at* http://legal.un.org/avl/ha/adp/adp.html.

32   The *Neer* case of 1926 is said by some commentators and advocates to encapsulate the level of protection that host States had to grant to foreign nationals. The case "asserted a high standard for the violation of the international minimal standard by requiring that the denial of justice must be such as would shock a reasonable bystander." *Neer v. United Mexican States*, 4 R. Int'l Arb. Awards 60, ¶ 1 (Mex-U.S. Cl. Comm'n Oct. 15, 1926).

33   *See* ADREAS F. LOWENFELD, INTERNATIONAL ECONOMIC LAW 469–470 (2nd ed. 2008).

34   Green H. Hackworth, 3 *Digest of International Law* 655 (1942) (emphasis added).

35   Bernardo M. Cremades, *Disputes Arising Out of Foreign Direct Investment in Latin America: A New Look at the Calvo Doctrine and Other Jurisdictional Issues*, 59 DISP. RES. J. 78, 80 (2004); *see also* Research in International Law, Harvard Law School, *The Law of Responsibility of States for Damage Done in Their Territory to the Person or Property of Foreigners*, 23 AM. J. INT'L L., SPECIAL SUPP. 131, 203 (1929) [hereinafter Draft Articles on State Responsibility] (providing a historical background on the Calvo Doctrine under the commentary of Article 17 of the rules).

Affairs—in response to Cordell Hull's letter regarding Mexico's expropriation of US property—essentially adhered to the Calvo Doctrine: "Your Excellency's Government insists [that] ... to expropriate, without just and prompt compensation, is confiscation.... Mexico considers that it is not in such a situation ... having done everything that it should in accordance with its own law ..."[36]

All of these doctrines, however, without the right to raise them before a competent tribunal would have very little impact in improving a foreign investor's situation. Individuals and companies had no standing under international law to sue a sovereign State before an international court or other authority.[37] From time to time, Governments espoused the grievances of their nationals against foreign States, effectively elevating such claims to the international law level as the home State's claim;[38] a practice, which is known as diplomatic protection or espousal.[39] As a precondition to invoke this remedy, the aggrieved nationals, however, needed to exhaust local remedies, by first litigating their

---

36 Letter from the Secretary of State of the United State to the Mexican Ambassador at Washington, *reprinted in Expropriation by Mexico of Agrarian Properties Owned by American Citizens*, 32 AM. J. INT'L L., SUPP. 181, 200 (1938). Elihu Root in his 1910 opening presidential address to the American Society of International Law explained the relation between minimum standard and national treatment: "There is a standard of justice, very simple, very fundamental, and of such general acceptance by all civilized countries as to form a part of the international law of the world. The condition upon which any country is entitled to measure the justice due from it to an alien by the justice which it accords to its own citizens is that its system of law and administration shall conform to this general standard. If any country's system of law and administration does not conform to that standard, although the people of the country may be content or compelled to live under it, no other country can be compelled to accept it as furnishing a satisfactory measure of treatment to its citizens." Elihu Root, *The Basis of Protection to Citizens Residing Abroad*, 4 AM. J. INT'L L. 517, 522 (1910).

37 Jaomijn J Van Hearsolte-Van Hof & Anne K Hoffmann, *The Relationship Between International Tribunals and Domestic Courts*, in THE OXFORD HANDBOOK ON INTERNATIONAL INVESTMENT LAW 963, 988–98 (Peter Muchlinski, Federico Ortino, & Christoph Schreuer eds., 2008) [hereinafter THE OXFORD HANDBOOK]; *see also* PARLETT, *supra* note 25, at 51.

38 The idea of diplomatic protection is built around the fiction proposal by Emeris de Vattel that "Whoever uses a citizen ill, indirectly offends the state, which is bound to protect this citizen; and the sovereign of the latter should avenge his wrongs, punish the aggressor, and, if possible, oblige him to make full reparation; since otherwise the citizen would not obtain the great end of the civil association, which is safety." E. VATTEL, THE LAW OF NATIONS, OR THE PRINCIPLES OF NATURAL LAW 298 (Béla Kapossy & Richard Whatmore eds. 2008); *see also* PARLETT, *supra* note 25, at 55.

39 EDWIN BORCHARD, THE DIPLOMATIC PROTECTION OF CITIZENS ABROAD 349 (1915); *see also* PARLETT, *supra* note 25, at 51–52, 55; August Reinisch & Loretta Malintoppi,

claims up to the highest level of local courts, unless such recourse would have been futile.[40] The foreign offices who received espousal requests had discretion to espouse such claims,[41] however, they may not necessarily have been sympathetic to such requests, given that it would pit their interests against those of a potentially friendly State.[42]

IV Protection through Peaceful Means of Settlement of Disputes: Hague Conferences, PCIJ, ICJ

With increased cross-border economic activity of nationals of industrialized nations abroad, the use of gunboat diplomacy and diplomatic espousal as tools to protect nationals abroad remained limited. As such, the international communities' focus gradually shifted to developing peaceful means of dispute settlement, including using international arbitration. The idea at the outset was to use such means to resolve State-to-State disputes.[43] Yet, the mechanism evolved to resolve disputes between States and private persons.[44] As early as

---

    Methods of Dispute Resolution, *in* THE OXFORD HANDBOOK, *supra* note 37, at 691, 712–13; AMERASINGHE, *supra* note 25, at 3 & n. 1, 28.

40 AMERASINGHE, *supra* note 25, at 3 & n. 1, 28. *See also* Don Wallace Jr., *Fair and Equitable Treatment and Denial of Justice: Loewen v US and Chattin v Mexico, in* INTERNATIONAL LAW AND ARBITRATION: LEADING CASES FROM THE ICSID, NAFTA, BILATERAL TREATIES AND CUSTOMARY INTERNATIONAL LAW 669, 672 (Todd Weiler ed., 2005); JAN PAULSSON, DENIAL OF JUSTICE IN INTERNATIONAL LAW 10 (2005); PARLETT, *supra* note 25, at 51.

41 *See* August Reinisch & Loretta Malintoppi, Methods of Dispute Resolution, *in* THE OXFORD HANDBOOK, *supra* note 37, at 713; *see also* Restatement (Third) of Foreign Relations Law § 902 (1987) ("*i. State claims deriving from injury to private persons.* Like other claims for violation of an international obligation, a state's claim for a violation that caused injury to rights or interests of private persons is a claim of the state and is under the state's control. The state may determine what international remedies to pursue, may abandon the claim, or settle it. The state may merge the claim with other claims with a view to an *en bloc* settlement. The claimant state may set these claims off against claims against it by the respondent state. Any reparation is, in principle, for the violation of the obligation to the state, and any payment made is to the state.").

42 BORCHARD, *supra* note 39, at 366.

43 AMERASINGHE, *supra* note 25, at 25, 28.

44 PARLETt, *supra* note 25, at 49.

the Jay Treaty of 1794,[45] or possibly earlier,[46] States started setting up international claims commissions, also known as mixed claims commissions,[47] to which claims by two States against each other, as well as those on behalf of their own nationals could be submitted.[48] These commissions also provided for the mass espousal of private persons' claims, as espousals on an individual basis were rare, and were particularly set up after major historical events such as revolutions.[49] At this stage, private persons still could not sue a State directly.[50] The 1899 and 1907 Hague peace conferences, which created the Permanent Court of Arbitration ("PCA"), were perhaps the first successful efforts at creating the blue print of a system that was later largely adapted to be used in disputes between States and foreign nationals.[51] Alongside the rise of the PCA, the first wave of ad hoc international arbitral disputes initiated based on arbitration clauses in major contracts were probably those against the Soviet Union in the early 1920s.[52]

---

45 Treaty of Amity, Commerce, and Navigation, Between His Britannic Majesty and the United States of America (Jay Treaty), US-U.K., Nov. 19, 1794, 8 Stat. 116, T.S. 105, 12 Bevans 13.

46 See AMERASINGHE, *supra* note 25, at 3 & n. 1, 28 (discussing the shifting trend by the end of the eighteenth century from reprisal to diplomatic protection or settlement by international arbitration). For a concise review of historical doctrines of reprisals and how they relate to modern concepts of denial of justice, minimum standard, and fair and equitable treatment see Wallace, *supra* note 40.

47 JACKSON HARVEY RALSTON, THE LAW AND PROCEDURE OF TRIBUNALS BEING A RÉSUMÉ OF THE VIEWS OF ARBITRATORS QUESTIONS ARISING UNDER THE LAW OF NATIONS 33 (Stanford University Press rev. ed. 1926); *see also* BORCHARD, *supra* note 39, at 296.

48 *See, e.g.*, RALSTON, *supra* note 47, at 34 (discussing the Alaska Boundary Commission).

49 PARLETT, *supra* note 25, at 55.

50 Id.

51 Jaomijn J Van Hearsolte-Van Hof & Anne K Hoffmann, *The Relationship Between International Tribunals and Domestic Courts*, *in* THE OXFORD HANDBOOK, *supra* note 37, at 963, 989.

52 The *Lena Goldfields* arbitration is well known in this era. The case involved a mining and transportation concession between the Soviet Government and an English company that operated in Siberia. Because of a change in the economic policy of the country, the Government withheld vital performance owed under the concession contract. The company initiated an arbitration under the concession agreement. Three months after arbitration commenced, the Soviet Union withdrew from the arbitration. The claimant obtained a massive monetary award that the Government never recognized. V.V. Veeder, *The Lena Goldfields Arbitration: The Historical Roots Of Three Ideas*, 47 INT'L & COMP. L.Q. 718, 747 (1998); *see also* Arthur Nussbaum, *Arbitration Between the Lena Goldfields Ltd. and the Soviet Government*, 36 CORNELL L. REV. 31, 32 (1950). Another example was the dispute

In the aftermath of the World War I, the Permanent Court of International Justice (or "PCIJ") was created in the context of the creation of the League of Nations. Some cases involving investment disputes, most prominently the *Chorzów Factory*[53] and *Mavrommatis Palestine Concession*,[54] were decided by this court. Both cases, however, were submitted through espousal. After WWII, the successor to the PCIJ, the International Court of Justice ("ICJ") has since ruled on a limited number of cases involving foreign investment, including the 1953 *Anglo Iranian Oil Co. Case*,[55] the *Barcelona Traction Case*,[56] and the 1987 *Case Concerning Elettronica Sicula S.P.A. (ELSI)*.[57]

V   Post-World War II: Promotion and Protection of Private Capital Flows

A   *Security for Foreign Investment through Investment Guarantees*

After WWII, one of the major efforts that the international community undertook was the creation of a comprehensive world trading system through a proposed international trade organization or "ITO". The Havana Charter of 1948[58] reflected this aspiration. The Charter emphasized the idea that foreign investment from both public and private sources was desirable for economic

---

with the Soviet Union over the Harriman concession involving rights to mine manganese deposits in Georgia. Stephen D. Fitch, *The Harriman Manganese Concession in the Soviet Union: Lessons for Today*, 9 INT'L TAX & BUS. L. 209, 209 (1991). Averell Harriman commenced arbitration under the concession, however, the dispute was settled without an award. Veeder, at 718.

53   *Case Concerning The Factory at Chorzow*, 1928 P.C.J.I. (ser. A) No. 17 (Sept. 13).
54   *The Mavrommatis Palestine Concessions*, 1924 P.C.J.I. (ser. A) No. 2 (Aug. 30).
55   *Anglo-Iranian Oil Co.* (U.K. v. Iran), 1952 I.C.J. 93 (July 22).
56   *Barcelona Traction Light and Power* (Belg. v. Spain) 1964 I.C.J. 6 (July 24).
57   *Elettronica Sicula S.p.A.* (ELSI) (U.S. v. It.), 1989 I.C.J. 15 (July 20).
58   The ITO was an American initiative as America was the dominant economic power after the WWII. In the first meeting of the U.N. Economic and Social Council (ECOSOC) in 1946, the United States called for the UN Convention on Trade and Employment to initiate the drafting of the ITO charter. The United States called for the convening of a United Nations Conference on Trade and Employment with the purpose of drafting a charter for an international trade organization. The preparatory work on the ITO charter began in the same year. It was concluded in 1948 at the Havana Conference. John H. Jackson, William J. Davey & Alan O. Sykes, Legal Problems of International Economic Relations 212–13 (4th ed. 2001) [hereinafter Legal Problems of International Economic Relations]; Havana Charter for an International Trade Organization, art. 1, U.N. Doc. E/Conf. 2/78, at 14 (Mar. 24, 1948) [hereinafter "Havana Charter"] ("REALIZING the aims net forth in the Charter of the United

development.[59] Ultimately, the post WWII world trading system did not include any discussion of investment protection norms mainly because no consensus was reached about the substance of the norms that would protect foreign nationals, including such fundamental concepts as the minimum standard itself.[60]

Faced with such political and legal hurdles, some developed countries started to establish investment guarantee programs to insure their nationals' investments against political risks.[61] The advantage of these guarantees is that it enabled investors claiming injury to deal with their own government, keeping them immune from "the actions of the country of investment."[62] The United States, for example, established in 1969 the Overseas Private Investment Corporation ("OPIC"), which allowed investors to purchase insurance from the federal government for losses arising from expropriation, among others. This program "for the first time provided expropriated investors with a source of recovery which was not dependent upon the agreement of the expropriating country to negotiate or the agreement of the U.S. government to espouse the claim."[63]

Nations, particularly the attainment of the higher standards of living, full employment and conditions of economic and social progress and development ....").

[59] One of the objectives of the Havana Charter was "[t]o foster and assist industrial and general economic development, particularly of those countries which are still in the early stages of industrial development, and to encourage the international flow of capital for productive investment." Havana Charter, *supra* note 58, art. 1(2). In addition, Article 12 recognizes that "the international flow of capital will be stimulated to the extent that Members afford nationals of other countries opportunities for investment and security for existing and future investments...." Id. art. 12.

[60] Developing countries, however, expressed hostility to some provisions of the charter, especially provisions related to the protection of FDI. In any case, the primary incentive for them to continue negotiations toward a final draft of the charter was to continue to receive development assistance from the United States. Once the United States lost interest in the ITO, developing countries also ceased supporting the initiative. DUGAN ET AL., *supra* note 26, at 48.

[61] Id. at 40.

[62] U.N. Secretary-General, *The Promotion of the International Flow of Private Capital*, ¶ 178, U.N. Doc. E/3325 (1960).

[63] Kenneth J. Vandevelde, *Reassessing the Hickenlooper Amendment*, 29 VA. J. INT'L L. 115, 123–24 (1988). Vandevelde further notes that: "The U.S. government does become involved to the extent of negotiating agreements with other countries in order to include those nations in the OPIC program. Further, in accordance with the agreements, the U.S. government, through OPIC, has the right to demand arbitration of the insured's claim, to which OPIC becomes subrogated as the insurer. Investors, however, are compensated

Moreover, as early as 1948, the World Bank sponsored multilateral discussions regarding the promotion of international investment through political risk insurance. After much discussion, negotiation, and numerous drafts, these talks led to the creation of Multilateral Investment Guarantee Agency (MIGA) under auspices of the World Bank.[64]

B *Security through Arbitration: Creation of the World Bank's International Centre for Settlement of Investment Disputes*[65]

The International Centre for Settlement of Investment Disputes ("ICSID") is the most frequently used modern international institution, which administers investment arbitration disputes. Its creation is partly a reflection of the international community's desire to protect foreign investment necessary for development through depoliticized dispute alternatives. The first such attempt involved creation of the ITO discussed earlier. The second was the Abs-Shawcross Draft Convention on Investments Abroad (1959), which was a private initiative. It provided for the automatic arbitration of investment disputes and included far-reaching rights for the unilateral enforcement of arbitral awards, which may have deterred developing countries from supporting the convention.[66] The convention, however, did not gain widespread governmental support. The third attempt was the Draft Convention on the Protection of Foreign Property by the Organization for Economic Co-operation and Development ("OECD"). The draft was negotiated in the 1960s and was a modification on the Abs-Shawcross draft.[67] This draft convention also failed because it was perceived as reflecting the interests of developed countries.[68]

Observing the mistakes of other conventions, the World Bank then took the initiative to draft a multilateral convention on investment. The World Bank

---

regardless of OPIC's decision to arbitrate or not to arbitrate. To the extent that the U.S. government through OPIC does pursue claims and obtain compensation, the investment insurance program may be regarded as an indirect remedy. But precisely to the extent that the program is a remedy, it is dependent upon the involvement of the U.S. government in the dispute." Id.

64 IBRAHIM F. I. SHIHATA, MIGA AND FOREIGN INVESTMENT (1988).
65 On history of ICSID Convention see Antonio Parra, The History of ICSID (Oxford 2012); Christoph Schreuer, Loretta Malintoppi, August Reinisch, and Anthony Sinclair, The ICSID Convention: A Commentary (2nd ed., Cambridge 2009). See also documents on the history of the negotiation of the ICSID Convention, *available at* https://icsid.worldbank.org/apps/ICSIDWEB/resources/Pages/The-History-of-the-ICSID-Convention.aspx.
66 Legal Problems of International Economic Relations, *supra* note 58, at 191.
67 OECD Draft Convention on Protection of Foreign Property, 7 I.L.M. 117 (1967).
68 Legal Problems of International Economic Relations, *supra* note 58, at 138.

was more successful than the OECD because its negotiations included more member states than the OECD and the discussions in the World Bank were economics-oriented and apolitical at the time. Further, the World Bank negotiations avoided addressing the sensitive issue of treatment of foreign property and compulsory adjudication of investment disputes. Rather, the use of the dispute resolution facilities was voluntary, both a State and an investor could submit a dispute to the relevant facility, and once a foreign investor submitted a dispute to international arbitration, it could not seek diplomatic protection from its home State. During the course of drafting the ICSID Convention, it was emphasized that "the parties [...] would not by the fact of their signature of or adherence to the Convention undertake any obligation to make use of these facilities in any specific area."[69] After several years of preparatory work, the World Bank presented to the member governments the convention for signature and ratification in March 1965. The Convention entered into force on September 14, 1966.

C   Contractual Techniques to Protect Foreign Investment

Parallel to these developments, transnational corporations and other capital exporters devised contractual techniques to protect their investments against various risks particularly in major projects involving extraction of natural resources. Such devices were primarily choice of law clauses, which included general principles of law or international law, stabilization clauses and international arbitration. Relying upon such theories, a number of arbitral tribunals, particularly during the 1950s–1970s in connection with nationalizations of oil concession in the Middle East, ruled that the underlying contracts were internationalized and hence would trump the local laws in case of inconsistency.[70] In one case, the local laws of an Islamic nation were deemed

---

69   Aron Broches, *Development of International Law by the International Bank for Reconstruction and Development*, *in* Proceedings of ASIL 33, 81 (1965); Paper prepared by the General Counsel and transmitted to the members of the Committee of the Whole, SID/63–2 (Feb. 18, 1963), *in* 2 THE HISTORY OF THE ICSID CONVENTION 72–73 (ICSID Publ'n reprint 2009) (1968).

70   Three cases were decided in the 1950s. These cases are *Petroleum Development (Trucial Coast) Ltd. v. Sheikh of Abu Dhabi* (1951) 18 I. L. R. 144; *Ruler of Qatar v. International Marine Oil. Co. Ltd*, (1953) 20. ILR 534; *Aramco v. Saudi Arabia* (1963) 27 ILR 117. The other three cases consisted of the three Libyan awards made in the 1970s. *See Libyan American Oil Company v Libyan Arab Republic*, 62 ILR 140 (April 12, 1977) ('LIAMCO'); *BP Exploration Co (Libya) Ltd. v. Government of the Libyan Arab Republic*, 53 ILR 297 300–357 (October 10,

immature to deal with petroleum concessions.[71] In looking outside the laws of the host states, arbitrators in these cases rationalized that contractual sanctity was the basic norm that applied to foreign investment contracts. This basic norm was identified as a general principle of law. Accordingly, through Article 38 of the ICJ, the principle of *pacta sunt servanda* was elevated to a general principle of international law. The principle, thus, provided the link between international law and foreign investment contracts.[72] This reasoning, however, is not without its critics.[73]

The above contractual devices gradually became the main method of protecting foreign investors prior to the advent of investment treaty-based protections.

D *The New International Economic Order (NIEO)*

In the 1960s, several former colonies gained their independence and joined the membership of the United Nations. With the inception of the Cold War, and the increased nationalization of foreign property around the world, new concerns arose in capital exporting nations regarding the security of international investment.[74] Capital exporting counties, in this era, took the position that expropriation has to be accompanied by prompt adequate and effective compensation mandated by the Hull formula. Developing countries, however, advocated among others a more relaxed compensation requirement. The debate ultimately was moved to the UN General Assembly ("UNGA").

Developing countries, using their superior numbers in the General Assembly (later known as Group of 77[75]) succeeded in passing a series of resolutions to

---

1973); *Texaco Overseas Petroleum Company and California Asiatic Oil Company v Government of Libya*, (Preliminary Award), 53 ILR 389 (Nov. 27, 1975).

71   SORNARAJAH, *supra* note 5, at 96.
72   Id. at 97.
73   Id. (critiquing this reasoning). *Aminoil v. Kuwait* was decided after the six cases undermined the internationalization theory and marked a change from the earlier cases. Government of the State of Kuwait v. The American Independent Oil Company (AMINOIL) 21 ILM 976 (March 24, 1982). SORNARAJAH, *supra* note 5, at 117–18; Rudolf Dolzer and Schreuer, *supra* note 15, at 75–77.
74   In 1951 Iran nationalized British oil assets. In 1955, Libya expropriated Liamco's concessions. A year later, Egypt nationalized the Suez Canal; and, late 1950s, Cuba nationalized the sugar industry. Zachary Elkins et. al., *Competing for Capital: The Diffusion of Bilateral Investment Treaties, 1960–2000*, 2008 U. ILL. L. REV. 265, 267 (2008).
75   *See generally* THE GROUP OF 77, http://www.g77.org/doc/ (last visited Oct. 30, 2015).

cement their general objectives. The first of these was UNGA Resolution 1803 (1962), which in the relevant part provided:

> 3. In cases where authorization is granted, the capital imported and the earning on that capital shall be governed by the terms thereof, by the national legislation in force, and by international law ...
> 4. Nationalization, expropriation or requisitioning shall be based on grounds or reasons of public utility, security or the national interest which are recognized as overriding purely individual or private interests, both domestic and foreign. In such cases the owner shall be paid appropriate compensation, in accordance with the rules in force in the State taking such measures in the exercise of its sovereignty and in accordance with international law....

In 1974, the UNGA released the Charter of Economic Rights and Duties of States (CERDS),[76] which envisaged preferential treatment for local capital. Capital exporting countries were not in favor of CERDS, and in particular did not support the notion that: "Every State has and shall freely exercise full permanent sovereignty, including possession, use and disposal, over all its wealth, natural resources and economic activities."[77] This notion was perceived to remove the act of nationalization from the protections of international law and was adopted over the objections of all the major capital-exporting nations.

Passage of these resolutions also raised the question whether the UNGA resolutions of the NIEO period had created new or changed norms of international law. Prof. Dupuy, who chaired the arbitration in *Texaco Overseas Petroleum Company v. Libyan Arab Republic* arbitration, held that out of all the resolutions adopted only Resolution 1803 "appears to a large extent as the expression of a real general will [of the nations]" but not CERDS.

In a way, the adoption of CERDS marked the tipping point of the NIEO.[78] In the subsequent years, the collapse of the Soviet Union (which was a source of ideological as well as material support for CERDS), and the conclusion of hundreds of BITs that included investment protections such as the Hull formula

---

76 G.A. Res. 3201 (S-VI), U.N. Doc. A/RES/S-6/3201 (May 1, 1974).
77 G.A. Res. 3281 (XXIX), U.N. Doc. A/9631 (Dec. 12, 1974).
78 DUGAN ET AL., *supra* note 26, at 25. *But see* SORNARAJAH, *supra* note 4, at 17 (arguing that the NIEOs influence persists to this day).

has largely rendered the relevance of the NIEO principles to the realm of the academy.[79]

VI FCN and BIT Programs and Recognition of Foreign Investor's Right to Directly Submit Claims to International Arbitration without Espousal or Exhaustion of Local Remedies

A Overview

It is widely recognized that Friendship, Commerce and Navigation ("FCN") treaties of the United States are forefathers of BITs.[80] The US FCN program started before WWII. In the aftermath of the war, these commercial treaties became an important tool in the articulation and implementation of US economic policy regarding standards of treatment and protection of US investments abroad.[81] These treaties include provisions that parallel modern BITs, including standards such as "equitable treatment" (the precursor to "fair and equitable treatment" in modern BITs), "most constant protection and security" (equivalent to "full protection and security" in modern BITs), and the prohibition of "unreasonable and discriminatory" treatment (mirroring "arbitrary and discriminatory measures" clauses in modern BITs). FCNs also contained clauses on expropriation that guaranteed prompt, adequate, and effective compensation.[82] These treaties, however, did not contain investor-State dispute resolution mechanics, although some of them provided that State-to-State

---

[79] Although, some commentators suggest that the NIEO movement, particularly Resolution 1803, may have had a more lasting impact. See World Bank, Report to the Development Committee and Guidelines on the Treatment of Foreign Direct Investment, 31 I.L.M. 1363, 1376 (1992).

[80] Kenneth J. Vandevelde, *The Bilateral Investment Treaty Program of the United States*, 21 CORNELL INT'L L.J. 201, 207 (1988) ("The modern FCNs contained antecedents to three of the four BIT core provisions.").

[81] K. Scott Gudgeon, *United States Bilateral Investment Treaties: Comments on Their Origin, Purposes, and General Treatment Standards*, 4 INT'L TAX & BUS. L. 105,107–108 (1986); *see also* ROBERT R. WILSON, UNITED STATES COMMERCIAL TREATIES AND INTERNATIONAL LAW (1960).

[82] Vandevelde, *supra* note 80, at 207. *See generally* Harry C. Hawkins, Commercial Treaties and Agreements: Principles and Practice (1951); R. WILSON, *supra* note 81; Herman Walker Jr., *Modern Treaties of Friendship, Commerce and Navigation*, 42 MINN. L. REV. 805 (1958).

disputes over the agreement's interpretation or application could be submitted to the ICJ.[83]

The US succeeded in concluding several of these treaties with a number of countries, particularly key trading partners of the US among developed economies.[84] However, due to their wide scope and complexity, the US did not succeed in attracting developing countries to conclude such treaties.[85]

European countries, however, took a number of steps to create a more watered down instrument by focusing only on the protection and promotion of foreign investment leaving out additional issues covered in traditional FCNs.[86] Abs and Shawcross spearheaded these efforts by preparing drafts of what later became the 1967 OECD Draft Convention on Protection of Foreign Property[87] and essentially a European Model BIT.[88]

Germany and Pakistan are generally viewed as having signed the first modern-style BIT in 1959 (although this treaty did not include investor-State dispute arbitration procedures). Other European countries quickly followed suit. In the four decades to follow, about 300 such treaties were negotiated.

B   Post-Cold War: Proliferation of BITs and Investment Treaty Disputes

With the end of the Cold War in 1989, many former socialist States (as well as other countries) gravitated to the western and capitalist prescriptions for managing economic affairs. BITs were an important part of the recipe, which purportedly was meant to attract foreign investment necessary to propel the stagnating economies of these countries towards industrialization and

---

83   Vandevelde, *supra* note 80, at 207 and n.53 (1988).
84   *See, e.g.*, Treaty of Friendship, Establishment and Navigation, Feb. 23, 1962, U.S.-Lu., art. XVII, 14 U.S.T. 251, T.I.A.S. No. 5306, at 12; Treaty of Friendship, Commerce and Navigation, Nov. 28, 1956, U.S.-S. Kor., art. XXIV, 8 U.S.T. 2217, T.I.A.S. No. 3947, at 17; Treaty of Friendship, Commerce and Navigation, Aug. 23, 1951, U.S.-Isr., art. XXIV, 5 U.S.T. 550, T.I.A.S. No. 2948, at 26.
85   Gudgeon, *supra* note 81, at 106–107.
86   Vandevelde, *supra* note 80, at 208 ("The European BIPAs differed from the modern FCNs in that they were concerned solely with investment protection.").
87   Chester Brown, *Introduction: The Development and Importance of the Model Bilateral Investment Treaty*, *in* COMMENTARIES ON SELECTED MODEL INVESTMENT TREATIES 7–8 (Chester Brown ed., 2013).
88   *See generally*, Georg Schwarzenberger, *The Abs-Shawcross Draft Convention on Investments Abroad: A Critical Commentary*, 9 J. PUB. L. 147 (1960).

efficiency. With these goals in mind, BITs rapidly proliferated with over 1400 treaties being concluded in the 1990s.[89]

Some economic studies have suggested that there is not a direct correlation between the conclusion of investment treaties and increased inflow of foreign investment.[90] Some scholars have attributed a "signalling effect" to conclusion of BITs considering them as important indicators of a State's willingness to protect foreign investment.[91] This idea of a correlation between BITs and the encouragement of foreign investment is supported by international financial institutions, such as the World Bank and the IMF, which have made the adoption of BITs among the conditions required for granting development loans.[92] Conclusion of BITs has coincided with the implementation of more fundamental economic policies including privatization of State-owned assets and enterprises across a variety of economic sectors in the 1990s, paving the way for the disputes that emerged in the following decade.

C   First Test of the Investment Treaty System: Early NAFTA and the Argentine Financial Crisis Cases

The first modern Arbitration, under the ICSID Convention and commenced under an investment treaty, was the *AAPL v. Sri Lanka*[93] in 1989. Then, in 1994

---

89   INVESTMENT POLICY HUB, http://investmentpolicyhub.unctad.org/IIA/Advanced SearchBITResults. During the same decade, however, an OECD initiative to conclude a Multilateral Agreement on Investment (MAI) did not succeed. See Jurgen Kurtz, *A General Investment Agreement in the WTO—Lessons from Chapter 11 of NAFTA and the OECD Multilateral Agreement on Investment*, 23 U. Pa. J. Int'l L. 756–761 (2002).

90   Lauge Skovgaard Poulsen, book review [K. Sauvant, and Lisa Sachs. (eds). *The Effect of Treaties on Foreign Direct Investment: Bilateral Investment Treaties, Double Taxation Treaties, and Investment Flows.*] Eur J Int Law (2009) 20 (3): 935–938 (asserting that the chapters of the books, which analyze studies to assess the impact of IIA on FDIs differ in their conclusions and suggesting that there is no consensus on the economic implications of IIAs); compare Matthias Busse, Jens Königer and Peter Nunnenkamp, FDI promotion through bilateral investment treaties: more than a bit?, Review of World Economics / Weltwirtschaftliches Archiv, Vol. 146, No. 1 (April 2010), pp. 147–177 (finding that BITs do promote FDI flow), with, Jason Webb Yackee, *Bilateral Investment Treaties, Credible Commitment, and the Rule of (International) Law: Do BITs Promote Foreign Direct Investment?*, 42 Law & Society Review 805 (2008) (finding no correlation between treaty protection and investment).

91   Thomas Wälde, 'The "Umbrella" Clause in Investment Arbitration: A Comment on Original Intentions and Recent Cases', 6 J. World Investment & Trade 183, 188 (2005).

92   SORNARAJAH, *supra* note 5, at 49.

93   *Asian Agricultural Products Ltd. (AAPL) v. Republic of Sri Lanka*; Case No. ARB/87/3, 30 ILM 577 (1991).

NAFTA came into force. Within three years of the ratification of NAFTA, several arbitrations were commenced under NAFTA Chapter 11 against all the NAFTA parties. The prospects of three independent arbitrators reviewing State measures and potentially contradicting the decisions of US courts was troublesome even for top lawyers. The other phenomena in this period was the increasing involvement of civil society groups and NGOs, which were very vocal about a variety of issues of public interest, such as the environment, public health, and democracy.[94]

NAFTA investors pushed the boundaries of protections as far as they could, asserting protections above and beyond the minimum standard of protection of aliens in customary international law leading the NAFTA parties to issue in 2001 Notes of Interpretation clarifying the limited nature of protections afforded under the so-called "fair and equitable treatment" standard.[95] The Notes of Interpretation also clarified and enhanced the transparency rules contained in NAFTA Chapter 11.[96] In 1999, Methanex brought the second NAFTA case against the US, seeking one billion dollars in damages.[97] Methanex challenged environmental regulation enacted by the Government of California as amounting to expropriation. Even though the UNCITRAL Arbitration Rules (which applied in that arbitration) provided for confidential proceedings, due to the public health issues surounding the case the disputing parties agreed to hold public hearings. This was viewed as a factor in the Free Trade Commission's decision to strenghten NAFTA's transparency rules. The Interpretative Notes require the parties' briefings and various communications in these cases be made publicly available, which provided an unprecedented opportunity to review and scrutinize these arbitral awards. The *Methanex* case was the first investment treaty arbitration that occurred in the public eye.

Meanwhile, in 2001–2002, the Argentine Republic experienced its worst economic crisis in decades, which was followed by a deluge of cases by foreign

---

[94] Don Wallace Jr., *Case Study under NAFTA: Lessons for the Wise?*, in ARBITRATING FOREIGN INVESTMENT DISPUTES: PROCEDURAL AND SUBSTANTIVE LEGAL ASPECTS, 237–264 (Stefan Michael Kroll and Norbert Horn eds. Kluwer Law International 2004).

[95] Notes of Interpretation of Certain Chapter 11 Provisions (NAFTA Free Trade Commission, July 31, 2001) *available at* <http://www.international.gc.ca/trade-agreements-accords-commerciaux/topics-domaines/disp-diff/NAFTA-Interpr.aspx?lang=eng>.

[96] North American Free Trade Agreement, Dec. 8-Dec.17, 1993, 32 I.L.M. 289, art. 1137 (4) & Annex 1137.2 (1993) (*hereinafter* NAFTA) (allowing the disputing parties to make public an award).

[97] *Methanex Corporation v. United States of America*, UNCITRAL Award (August 3rd, 2005) (challenging the Government of California's decision to ban a toxic gasoline additive as amounting to breach of the NAFTA).

investors who had invested in Argentine utilities and other sectors during the privatization. In spite of the flood of cases against Argentina, the continued adoption of investment treaties by other nations was not slowed. In 2004, the US updated its BIT model with the aim of incorporating legal developments in and outside NAFTA. The 2004 Model BIT reinvigorated the government's regulatory authority to address public interest concerns, which had been a source of tension during the early years of NAFTA.[98] In 2012, a new model BIT with additional changes was adopted. Following the US practice, other countries developed their own model BITs in order to facilitate the negotiation of investment agreements and secure concistency in their treatment of foreign investment.

Efforts at the regional level to create comprehensive investment regimes post-NAFTA have included the conclusion of DR-CAFTA,[99] ASEAN Comprehensive Investment Agreement,[100] and more recently the Trans-Pacific Partnership ("TPP"). The Energy Charter Treaty ("ECT") is another multilateral treaty aiming at the protection of investments in the energy sector. Like NAFTA, it was concluded in the 1990s and provides for investor-State dispute resolution mechanism.[101] Due to the impact of NAFTA and other investment treaty arbitrations, foreign investors have also started exploring and bringing claims under a number of other older agreements such as Organization of Islamic Conference Investment Agreement, Unified Agreement for Protection of Arab Capital, and the European Development Fund, all of which have been used to directly sue the host States of an investment.

VII   Content of Modern BITs

BITs—and investment chapters of free trade agreements—have some standard features and are generally similar in their organization and content. In general, BITs address four core substantive issues or protections: (1) methods for investment dispute resolution, (2) conditions for market access or the

---

98   *See* US Model BIT 2004 Annex B paragraph 4 (b) (stating that non-discriminatory regulatory measures aimed at protecting public health, safety and the environment do not amount to indirect expropriation).

99   Dominican Republic-Central America FTA (CAFTA), the entering into force depends on the particular country and ranges from 2006 to 2009.

100 Association of Southeast Nations (ASEAN) Comprehensive Investment Agreement, (26 Feb. 2009) in force since February 24th 2012.

101 Energy Charter Treaty, 2080 UNTS 95 (1994).

admission of foreign investors to the host State; (3) standards of treatment of foreign investors; and (4) compensation for expropriation.

A   Investor's Right to Directly Initiate Arbitration and the Idea of Unilateral Consent

The singular and revolutionary feature of the modern BIT is the direct right of foreign investors to commence international arbitration against host states of the investment, without requiring espousal by their home state or the exhaustion of local remedies. The basic underlying idea is that States provide a standing offer or a unilateral consent[102] for arbitration, which can be accepted at any time by a qualified investor, thereby creating a binding arbitration agreement.

This feature of treaties has sparked significant debate, in particular with how it touches upon such fundamental concepts as whether individuals are subjects of international law.[103] Other issues include whether the right to bring a claim belongs to foreign investors with the implication that it can be waived or it is simply a type of mass espousal of potential claims by the home State, in which the investor does not own such rights.[104]

---

102   Jan Paulsson in his now classic 1995 article called this type of arbitration "arbitration without privity". Jan Paulsson, *Arbitration without Privity*, ICSID Review (1995) 10 (2): 232–257. *See also* Christoph Schreuer, Consent to Arbitration *in* THE OXFORD HANDBOOK, *supra* note 37, at 835 (discussing consent through bilateral investment treaties in which the state parties to the BITs offer consent to arbitration to foreign investors who are nationals of the other contracting party and the arbitration agreement is perfected by acceptance of the offer by an illegible investor); Andrea Marco Steingruber, Consent in International Arbitration (Oxford 2012).

103   Similar rights of bringing claims had been granted to individuals under various human rights treaties. *See* David Sloss, *The Domestication of International Human Rights: Non-Self-Executing Declarations and Human Rights Treaties*, 24 Yale J. Int'l L. 129, 151–2 (1999) (discussing private right of action under human rights treaties).

104   Arthur W. Rovine asserts that the rights of investors under NAFTA are their own rights and not the rights of the state. *Americas, Inc. v. The United Mexican States*, ICSID Case No. ARB (AF)/04/5 (Rovine Separate Opinion, 20 September 2007) ("As with NAFTA, there is no indication that the claimant is enforcing the rights of the state. The language is significant in referring to a claimed breach of an "obligation" owed by the state Party to the investor. There is nothing regarding rights of states Parties, procedural rights, or derivative rights. There is no indication of diplomatic protection through claims espousal. There is no indication that States are protecting their nationals. Rather, nationals are protecting themselves by invoking their right to go to arbitration, pursuant to the treaties, to enforce State Party obligations owed to them.").

B   *Admission and Establishment*

One of the critical issues in most BITs is the market access or entry rights that such treaties accord to foreign investors. Under international law, States are free to prevent entry and access to their territory and market.[105] Market access, however, is a key objective of investment and trading systems, as it allows foreigners to sell their product and services in new territories. That process naturally creates competition for the local economic players who may or may not be able to withstand such external pressure.[106] The decision to allow market access is effected through treaty provisions on admission and establishment.[107]

Admission refers to the right of entry for investment into the host State market.[108] The right of establishment, however, refers to the conditions and the way the activity of the investor will take place over the duration of the investment. It entails the right to carry out business transactions and the right to set up a business presence.[109]

By and large, the great majority of investment treaties, particularly those following the European Model do not grant preferential treatment to the pre-establishment phases of an investment, and hence, no protection to rights of access.[110] National treatment (NT) and MFN treatment are only accorded to "operation, management, maintenance, use, enjoyment or disposal by such

---

105   James Crawford, Brownlie's Principles of Public International Law 609 (8th ed. 2012).
106   UNCTAD, WORLD INVESTMENT REPORT—FOREIGN DIRECT INVESTMENT AND THE CHALLENGE OF DEVELOPMENT, 174 (1999), *available at* http://unctad.org/en/Docs/wir1999_en.pdf ("[FDI] can also have a number of negative effects, such as crowding out domestic investors...."); UNCTAD, Admission and Establishment *in* UNCTAD SERIES ON ISSUES IN INTERNATIONAL INVESTMENT AGREEMENTS 38 (2002) (*hereinafter* Admission and Establishment) (discussing the economic and development impact of FDI and the policy choices of host countries including that "host countries may prefer to protect infant industries and domestic producers deemed not strong enough to compete with foreign firms.").
107   UNCTAD, Admission and Establishment, *supra* note 106; *see also* Ignacio Gómez-Palacio & Peter Muchlinski, *Admission and Establishment, in* THE OXFORD HANDBOOK, *supra* note 37, at 227, 229–30 (discussing the difference between the concept of establishment, admission, and market access); Rudolf Dolzer & Margrete Stevens, Bilateral Investment Treaties 50 (1995); see also most recently Armand de Mestral, *Pre-Entry Obligations under International Law*, in International Investment Law (Bungenberg, Griebel, Hobe, Reinisch eds., CH Beck Hart Nomos 2015), p. 685.
108   Ignacio Gómez-Palacio & Peter Muchlinski, *Admission and Establishment, in* THE OXFORD HANDBOOK, *supra* note 37, at 227, 230.
109   UNCTAD, Admission and Establishment, *supra* note 106, at 12.
110   *See* Marie-France Houde, *Novel Features in Recent OECD Bilateral Investment Treaties, in* International Investment Perspectives 143, 151–52 (2006) (distinguishing the European

investors ..." but not to "acquisition, expansion, and establishment of investment." Accordingly, entry is subject to compliance with local laws which may treat foreign investment in a discriminatory manner.

By contrast, the US investment treaties (as well as Canadian and Japanese treaties) grant limited right of access and protections—NT and MFN[111]—to foreign investors who seek to make an investment in the territory of a BIT contracting party.[112] Article 1102 of NAFTA for example, provides in the relevant part that:

> [e]ach Party shall accord to investments of investors of another Party treatment no less favorable than that it accords, in like circumstances, to investments of its own investors with *respect to the establishment, acquisition, expansion,* management, conduct, operation, and sale or other disposition of investments.[113]

Accordingly, the Parties to US-type treaties undertake not to discriminate on the basis of nationality if a foreign investor intends to make an investment in their territory.[114] That concession is presumably to provide an additional incentive for foreign investors to risk investing in the relevant State.[115]

Most recently, the provisions of Canada-EU Trade Agreement (CETA)[116] have adopted a US-type approach by granting NT and MFN in the pre-entry stage,[117] which is a major policy shift on the part of the EU. Market access rights

---

BITS and American BITS); Marie-France Houde & K. Yannaca-Small, *Relationships between International Investment Agreements* 4 (OECD Publ'n, Working Paper No. 1, 2004).

111   These two standards are further discussed below.
112   *See* Marie-France Houde, *supra* note 110, at 152.
113   NAFTA, *supra* note 96, art. 1102.
114   *See Most-Favored-Nation Treatment: A Sequel, in* UNCTAD SERIES ON ISSUES IN INTERNATIONAL INVESTMENT AGREEMENTS II 42 (2010) ("Pre-establishment covers the entry phase, which means that host States may not apply any discriminatory measure between foreigners as far as the entry conditions of the investor are concerned. This has a major implication: host States are not only prevented from applying any existing measure which is inconsistent with MFN treatment but also from creating a new one.").
115   Id. at 1–2.
116   EUROPEAN COMM'N, CONSOLIDATED CETA TEXT (2014) [hereinafter CA-EU CETA], *available at* http://trade.ec.europa.eu/doclib/docs/2014/september/tradoc_152806.pdf.
117   *See* Nathalie Bernasconi-Osterwalder, *The Draft Investment Chapter of the Canada-EU Comprehensive Economic and Trade Agreement: A Step Backwards for the EU and Canada?,* INVESTMENT TREATY NEWS (June 26, 2013); *see also* ELFRIEDE BIERBRAUER, DIRECTORATE-GEN. FOR EXTERNAL POLICIES, EUROPEAN PARLIAMENT, NEGOTIATIONS ON THE EU-CANADA COMPREHENSIVE ECONOMIC AND TRADE

however are rarely litigated in investor-State arbitration disputes, which is perhaps why the EU has consented to these obligations.[118]

C Key Substantive Protections for Foreign Investors

Modern BITs grant several substantive protections to foreign investors, including protection against expropriation without compensation, fair and equitable treatment ("FET"), MFN, NT, and Umbrella Clauses. A summary of the most prominent substantive provisions are detailed below.

Expropriation

Expropriation is the taking of privately-owned property by a State. State's have an inherent right under international law to expropriate property of foreign nationals, provided that it is for a public purpose, carried out in a non-discriminatory manner, in accordance with due process, and on payment of compensation. Such payment should approximate the fair market value of the expropriated asset immediately before the taking or before the taking was publicly known. Modern investment treaties generally recognize this right and these elements.[119] They also recognize that expropriation may be direct through outright physical seizure of property or through more subtle measures including regulation that affects the economic value of an investment or deprives the investor from the use or enjoyment of the investment.

While a direct expropriation is easy to identify, an indirect one is more complex. In recent years, the U.S. and other countries have tried to bring some measure of clarity by identifying criteria that may be used to determine whether an indirect expropriation has taken place, particularly when, and if

---

AGREEMENT (CETA) CONCLUDED 7 (2014) ("The agreement's investment chapter covers the establishment and protection of investors and investments at both central and sub-central government levels").

118 It is important to note that the investor-State Dispute Settlement mechanism in CETA is limited to breaches of few investment provisions such as non-discrimination, expropriation, and fair and equitable treatment. Investor-State dispute settlement cannot be used to by investors to claim a breach of other provisions of the agreement such as obtaining market access. CA-EU CETA, *supra* note 116, art. X.17; *see also* EUROPEAN COMMISSION, INVESTMENT PROVISIONS IN THE EU-CANADA FREE TRADE AGREEMENT (CETA) 4 (2014), *available at* http://trade.ec.europa.eu/doclib/docs/2013/november/tradoc_151918.pdf; Armand de Mestral, *When Does the Exception Become the Rule? Conserving Regulatory Space under CETA*, 18 J. INT'L ECON. L. 641, 643 (2015).

119 UNCTAD, *Expropriation: A Sequel*, *in* UNCTAD SERIES ON ISSUES IN INTERNATIONAL INVESTMENT AGREEMENTS II, at xii (2012).

regulatory measures may amount to an expropriation.[120] Some treaties specifically mention that measures adopted for protection of public interest in connection with health, environment, and sometimes taxation cannot amount to expropriation.[121] But, other treaties do not specifically address these issues and have led to initiation of claims such as those against Uruguay and Australia in connection with measures curtailing tobacco companies' trademark rights.

NT and MFN

NT and MFN prohibit discrimination against foreign investors due to their nationality. NT requires that foreign investors receive the same treatment as similarly situated local investors. Similarly, MFN requires that the foreign investor be treated no less favorably than investors from any third country. In order to determine whether such standards have been breached, one has to first identify a proper comparator; that is a person or entity that is similarly situated to the foreign investor, and then, determine whether the comparator has been treated better than the foreign investor, and if so, whether the State had a legitimate reason to do so.[122]

Attempts to apply the MFN to procedural rights which would enable foreign investors for example, to expand the scope of dispute resolution provisions of a treaty or bypass waiting periods under investment treaties, have been a controversial topic in recent years, particularly in the wake of the *Maffezini v. Spain* case.[123] The *Maffezini* tribunal upheld the right to rely on the MFN provision of the Argentina–Spain BIT to import the dispute resolution clause of the Chile–Spain BIT, which ultimately granted the tribunal jurisdiction to

---

120   *See, e.g.*, Annex B Article 4 (b) to U.S. Model BIT 2012.

121   *See e.g.*, The Common Market for Eastern and Southern Africa (COMESA) Investment Agreement (2007) Article 20 (8); ASEAN Comprehensive Investment Agreement, *supra* note 100, Annex 2(4); EU-Singapore FTA (2015) Paragraph 2 Annex 9-A; CA-EU CETA, *supra* note 116, Annex VIII-A (3).

122   *See* Todd J. Grierson-Weiler & Ian A. Laird, *Standards of Treatments*, *in* THE OXFORD HANDBOOK, *supra* note 37. NT and MFN typically extend to the treatment of foreign investors once and investment has been made. However, some American, Canadian and Japanese treaties extend these protections during the pre-entry stage too. UNCTAD, *National Treatment*, *in* UNCTAD SERIES ON ISSUES IN INTERNATIONAL INVESTMENT AGREEMENTS II, at xi (1999); UNCTAD, *Most-Favoured Nation Treatment*, *in* UNCTAD SERIES ON ISSUES IN INTERNATIONAL INVESTMENT AGREEMENTS II, at xiv (2010).

123   *Maffezini v. Spain*, ICSID Case No. ARB/97/7 (Jan. 25, 2000), 5 ICSID Rep. 396 (2002); see also the International Law Commission, Study Group on the Most-Favoured-Nation clause, UN Doc. A/70/10.

hear the dispute. More recent investment treaties have rejected the *Maffezini* approach and prohibited the incorporation of a dispute resolution clause of another treaty concluded by the Party concerned.[124] UNCITRAL and ICSID tribunals are, nevertheless, receptive to the expansion of substantive protections, such as a broader fair and equitable treatment standard, by means of the MFN clause.[125]

Fair and Equitable Treatment, Full Protection and Security and the Minimum Standard[126]

Fair and equitable treatment ('FET') has probably been the most invoked standard of treatment in recent years. Its broad terms have allowed foreign investors to argue that it requires a state to act consistently and reasonably, abstain from arbitrariness and discrimination, ensure due process, and ensure the protection of the legitimate expectation of investors.[127] Attempts have also been made to read into this provision a requirement of stability by reference to the preamble of some treaties, which specify that FET is necessary for providing a stable legal and commercial environment. The element of legitimate expectations features prominently in the application of FET, as it requires a foreign investor to show that it had relied on representations—in the form of laws, contractual provisions, and other statements—of the host State in order to invest capital, but the host State later changed course, frustrating the investor's expectations. In *AES* v. Hungary, the tribunal clarified whether

---

124 See e.g. U.S.-Colombia Trade Promotion Agreement (2006) n. 2 (excluding application of the MFN provision to dispute resolution mechanisms that are provided for in international investment treaties); U.S.-Peru Trade Promotion Agreement (2006) n.2 (same); Trans-Pacific Partnership (TPP) Agreement (Opened for signature February 4 2016, not yet in effect) Art. 9.5.3 (same); CA-EU CETA, *supra* note 116, Art. 8.7.4. (same).

125 See e.g. *Bayindir Insaat Turizm Ticaret Ve Sanayi A.S. v. Islamic Republic of Pakistan*, ICSID Case No. ARB/03/29, IIC 27 (2005), Decision on Jurisdiction, ¶¶ 231–232 (November 14th, 2005) (incorporating the FET standard via the MFN clause); *MTD Equity Sdn. Bhd. and MTD Chile S.A. v. Republic of Chile*, ICSID Case No. ARB/01/7, IIC 174, Award, ¶¶ 100–104 (May 25th, 2004) (importing a more favorable FET standard by means of MFN); *CME Czech Republic B.V. v. The Czech Republic*, Ad hoc Tribunal (UNCITRAL) Final award and separate opinion, ¶ 500 (March 14th, 2003) (importing notion of just compensation through an MFN provision).

126 See generally DUGAN ET AL., *supra* note 26, at 491.

127 UNCTAD, *Fair and Equitable Treatment, in* UNCTAD SERIES ON ISSUES IN INTERNATIONAL INVESTMENT AGREEMENTS II, at xiii (2012).

the FET standard required legal stability.[128] The tribunal stated that "'any reasonably informed business person or investor knows that laws can evolve in accordance with the perceived political or policy dictates of the times".[129] It was found that, as a result, the FET standard had not been breached. However, this issue remains unsettled.

Numerous attempts have been made to define how legitimate expectations are created. Thomas Wälde, in his dissenting opinion in Thunderbird, tried to show that the principle was essentially a general principle of law, similar to estoppel and *venire contra factum* with roots in the general principle of good faith. Others have argued that the concept is too unclear to be the basis of finding a treaty violation and nothing less than concrete legal commitments should create rights in foreign investors.

NAFTA States, in the aftermath of foreign investors' broad interpretations of this principle, have tried to curtail its scope by limiting it to the customary international law minimum standard for protection of aliens. The most dramatic attempt to define the scope of FET has been in CETA, which details the content of the obligation by listing the measures amounting to breach of the FET standard.[130] Together with FET, many investment treaties require States to accord foreign investors and their investment, full protection and security, which traditionally have required protecting the physical security of foreign nationals and their property. In recent years, it has been suggested that the standard may also be used to protect IP rights against web-based piracy.

Other Provisions

Many investment treaties contain so-called umbrella clauses, which require host States to honor any commitments to which they have entered into with respect to an investment.[131] It has been suggested that the standard elevates an ordinary breach of contract or municipal law into a breach of international law. Its application has been subject to a significant amount of litigation with mixed success for foreign investors.[132] Modern US treaties have eliminated the

---

128 AES *Summit Generation Limited and* AES-*Tisza Erömü Kft v. The Republic of Hungary*, ICSID Case No. ARB/07/22, IIC 455 (2010), Award (17 September, 2010).

129 Id. ¶ 9.3.34.

130 CA-EU CETA, *supra* note 116, Art. 8.10 (2).

131 Agreement Between the Government of Japan and the Government of the Russian Federation Concerning the Promotion and Protection of Investment, Japan-Russ., art. 3(3), Nov. 13, 1998.

132 *See* DUGAN ET AL., *supra* note 26, at 541. Nevertheless, in two decisions, SGS *v. Pakistan* and SGS *v. Philippines*, the tribunal refused to extend the jurisdiction of the tribunal to contract disputes under the umbrella clause. In SGS *v. Pakistan* the tribunal held that it

provisions and have included other provisions for protection of investment contracts and licenses.

D Key Aspects of the Investor State-Arbitration Process

The process of investor-State arbitration is, by and large, similar to international commercial arbitration, possibly due to the influence of international commercial arbitration lawyers in the field. Increasingly, this process is becoming more complex, lengthy, and costly, which is perhaps an antithesis of the idea of arbitration. The influence of American-style litigation techniques may be partly responsible for this.[133] But the reality is that investment treaty disputes commonly involve major investment projects and sensitive issues, which requires a measured approach to litigation.

Arbitral Rules and Organization of Process

The arbitral process is governed by the rules of arbitration designated under a BIT and then chosen usually by the claimant when it submits the dispute. The most commonly used rules are those of ICSID and the UNCITRAL Arbitration rules used in *ad hoc* arbitration. Both ICSID and UNCITRAL Rules, during the past decade, have gone through changes in order to better adapt to the investor-State arbitration process. The process under both set of rules is flexible. The major difference may be that the ICSID Convention is a self-contained system whereby all aspects of a dispute are handled pursuant to the ICSID rules, including the annulment of awards. By contrast, under the UNCITRAL Arbitration Rules, recourse to local courts would be necessary to set aside or annul an award under the 1958 New York Convention.

---

does not have jurisdiction over contractual claims on the ground that umbrella clauses do not in general extend to such claims. Société Général de Surveillance S.A. v. Pakistan, ICSID Case No. ARB/01/13, Objections to Jurisdiction, ¶¶ 163–74 (Aug. 5, 2003), 18 ICSID Rev. 301 (2003). In *SGS v. Philippines*, tribunal decided that it has such jurisdiction, but determine that it should not exercise this jurisdiction where the contract contains an exclusive forum selection clause designating a different forum for resolving disputes arising under the contract. Société Général de Surveillance S.A. v. Philippines, ICSID Case No. ARB/02/6, Objections to Jurisdiction, ¶¶ 113–29, 136–55 (Jan. 29, 2004), 8 ICSID Rep. 518 (2005). *See also* Jarrod Wong, 'Umbrella Clauses in Bilateral Investment Treaties: Of Breaches of Contract, Treaty Violations, and the Divide Between Developing and Developed Countries in Foreign Investment Disputes', Geo. Mason L. Rev. 135, 137 (2006).

133 Eric Bergsten, *Americanization of International Arbitration*, 18 PACE INT'L L. REV. 289, 294 (2006) ("American lawyers participating in international commercial arbitration brought and used American litigation skills.").

Selection and Challenge of Arbitrators

Arbitral panels generally consist of two party-appointed arbitrators and a chairperson who may be appointed either by the agreement of the parties, by the two party-appointed arbitrators or by an appointing authority. Choosing the optimal candidate for party-appointed arbitrator has become an increasingly complex process and has attracted criticism. It is a fundamental tenet of arbitration that all arbitrators are independent and impartial, and it is presumed that all arbitrators possess these qualities. Parties naturally tend to select an arbitrator with what they perceive is a predisposition towards them in terms of legal or cultural background or having doctrinal views that coincide with the selecting party. Such a predisposition is not a disqualifying attribute so long as the arbitrator is conscious of this fact and does not allow it to override his professional judgment.[134] Others feel differently and consider such predisposition as a positive bias and severely criticize the process of party-appointment in investor-State disputes.[135] Those critics advocate for a non-party selection process.

Critical to the process is the arbitrator's role after they are selected.[136] They must act in an independent manner in order to ensure fair treatment to the parties during the arbitral proceedings.[137] In order to guarantee the arbitrator's independence, they are required to disclose information and circumstances that could reasonably lead to disqualification, such as any legal advice or expert opinion on the dispute provided to a party.[138] Each institution has its own grounds for the disqualification of arbitrators; however, all consider

---

134   R. Doak Bishop & Lucy Reed, *Practical Guidelines for Interviewing, Selecting and Challenging Party-Appointed Arbitrators in International Commercial Arbitration*, 14 Arb. Int'l 2 (1998) *available at* http://www.nadr.co.uk/articles/published/arbitration/SelectingArbitrators.pdf.

135   *See generally* Jan Paulsson, *Moral Hazard in International Dispute Resolution*, TDM, June 10, 2010. *See also* Kahale, at note 196 *infra*.

136   Lowenfeld, *supra* note 33, at 60.

137   *See e.g.* Convention on the Settlement of Investment Disputes between States and Nationals of Other States *adopted* Mar. 18, 1965, 575 U.N.T.S. 159 [hereinafter ICSID Convention] Article 14 stating that: "Persons designated to serve on the Panels shall be persons of high moral character and recognized competence in the fields of law, commerce, industry or finance, who may be relied upon to exercise independent judgment."

138   International Bar Association (IBA) Guidelines on Conflicts of Interests in International Arbitration (October 23, 2014) (*hereinafter* 2014 IBA Guidelines) Section 2.1.1. Waivable Red List.

grounds leading to justifiable doubts as to the arbitrator's impartiality and independence sufficient for disqualification.[139] The 2014 IBA Guidelines, although a non-binding instrument, has been commonly referenced when making a determination on an arbitrator's disqualification.

One of the grounds invoked for disqualification is the repeated appointment of an arbitrator by a party. In *Burlington v. Ecuador*, the defendant claimed that the lack of disclosure of the arbitrator's repeated appointment by the claimant's law firm was a ground for recusal.[140] However, it was the arbitrator's conduct in response to Ecuador's questioning during the disqualification procedure that resulted in his removal.[141] In another case, *Tidewater v. Venezuela*, the claimant's request for the disqualification of an arbitrator was rejected after finding that, although the arbitrator failed to disclose repeated appointments by Venezuela, the arbitrator had rendered decisions against Venezuela in previous cases.[142] The decision to disqualify an arbitrator is factually driven and decided on a case-by-case basis. ICSID tribunals have clarified that the *appearance* of dependence or bias, rather than actual dependence or bias, suffices to warrant the disqualification of arbitrators.[143] ICSID tribunals have, therefore, departed from their previous higher threshold, which required "obvious" or "highly probable" bias.[144]

Other grounds for the disqualification of an arbitrator are: the arbitrator's pre-conceived position outside the context of a case, such as academic writings, giving the impression of conflict with the subject matter of the dispute;

---

139   See e.g. UNCITRAL Arbitration Rules, Article 12, G.A. Res. 65/22, UN Doc. A/RES/65/22 (2010) (*hereinafter* 2010 UNCITRAL Rules) ("Any arbitrator may be challenged if circumstances exist that give rise to justifiable doubts as to the arbitrator's impartiality or independence."); ICSID Convention, *supra* note 137, Article 57 ("A party may propose to a Commission or Tribunal the disqualification of any of its members on account of any fact indicating a manifest lack of the qualities required by paragraph (1) of Article 14).

140   See *Burlington Resources Inc. v. Republic of Ecuador*, ICSID Case No. ARB/08/5, Decision on the Proposal for Disqualification of Professor Francisco Orrego Vicuña, ¶ 70 (13 Dec. 2013) (*hereinafter* Burlington's Decision on the Proposal for Disqualification).

141   Id. ¶ 79.

142   *Tidewater Inc., Tidewater Investment SRL, Tidewater Caribe, C.A., et al.* v. The Bolivarian Republic of Venezuela, ICSID Case No. ARB/10/5, Decision on Claimants' Proposal to Disqualify Professor Brigitte Stern, Arbitrator, ¶ 64 (23 Dec. 2010).

143   Burlington's Decision on the Proposal for Disqualification, *supra* note 140, ¶¶ 75, 78–80.

144   Chiara Giorgetti, *Between Legitimacy and Control: Challenges and Recusals of Judges and Arbitrators in International Courts and Tribunals*, 49 Geo. Wash. Int'l L. Rev 205, 217, 219 (2017).

improper conduct during the proceedings; and the so-called "double hatting".[145] 'Double hatting' in international arbitration is the practice by which a practitioner performs roles of arbitrator, counsel and expert witness in other or subsequent investment proceedings. For example, a practitioner may advocate a particular view on a legal issue when acting as counsel in one case, and rule on the same issue when simultaneously acting as arbitrator in another case.

Each arbitral institution provides its own procedural mechanism for challenging an arbitrator. UNCITRAL requires that a challenge be brought within 15 days,[146] and empowers a third party, the "appointing authority", to decide on the challenge.[147] ICSID instead analyses the timeliness of the challenge on a case-by-case basis, and empowers the remaining members of the tribunal to decide the challenge.[148] The Permanent Court of Arbitration (PCA) provides 30 days after the party became aware of the circumstances giving rise to the challenge,[149] and refers the issue to the "appointing authority" for final determination.[150]

The right to challenge the impartiality of an arbitrator, in principle, grants the disputing parties control over the composition of the tribunal, and more broadly, contributes to the legitimacy of investor-State arbitration. That said, there are some questions as to whether the current system has implemented *effective* mechanisms and institutional safeguards.[151] The failure to guarantee the impartiality of arbitrators has been one of the strongest criticisms of investor-State arbitration, especially of ICSID, which gives the unchallenged members of the tribunal the authority to assess the impartiality of their peers.[152]

---

145   Id. at 228–229.
146   2010 UNCITRAL Rules, *supra* note 139, art. 13.1.
147   Id. art. 13.4.
148   ICSID Convention, *supra* note 137, art. 58. The Chairman of the ICSID's Administrative Council steps in if the member(s) of the tribunal are unable to reach a decision concerning challenge of the arbitrator.
149   Permanent Court of Arbitration (PCA) Arbitration Rules (2012) art. 13.1.
150   Id. art. 13.4 (providing that the Appointing Authority is the Secretary General of the PCA).
151   *See generally* The Backlash against Investment Arbitration: Perceptions and Reality (Michael Waibel et al. eds., Kluwer Law, 2010).
152   Chiara Giorgetti, *supra* note 144, at 237.

Governing Law, Interpretation Tools, and Role of Precedent

Some investment treaties have choice of law provisions, which enumerate the sources of law to be consulted requiring application of host State, international law, as well as other sources such as any relevant agreements.[153] In the absence of such provisions, in an ICSID arbitration Article 42 of the ICSID Convention provides for the application of the law agreed upon by the parties, or if there is no such law, then the law of the Contracting State party to the dispute (including its conflicts of law rules) *and* international law.[154] In an UNCITRAL case, the issue will be decided pursuant to Article 33, which provides that failing an agreement between the parties, the tribunal shall apply the law that it determines is appropriate.[155] UNCITRAL tribunals have not until recently addressed the issue of applicable law when a treaty is silent. Traditionally, arbitral tribunals have relied on principles such as supremacy of international over national law to resolve conflicts. In recent years, however, there has been a move to clarify some fundamental issues such as the principle that the scope of property rights of a foreign investor has to be determined by reference to local law.[156]

Arbitral tribunals usually rely on the general tools of treaty interpretation particularly the Vienna Convention on the Law of Treaties (VCLT) Article 31 and 32 to interpret BIT provisions.[157] They also rely on canons of treaty

---

153 For instance, Netherlands-Czech Republic BIT provides that "the tribunal shall decide on the basis of law taking into account the law of the host country concerned, parties' agreements, and general principles of international law."

154 ICSID Convention, *supra* note 137, art. 42. For a comprehensive recent treatment of the subject see HEGE ELISABETH KJOS, APPLICABLE LAW IN INVESTOR-STATE ARBITRATION: THE INTERPLAY BETWEEN NATIONAL AND INTERNATIONAL LAW (Oxford University Press 2013).

155 2010 UNCITRAL Rules, *supra* note 139, art. 33.

156 K. Lipstein, *Conflict of Laws before International Tribunals* (ii), 29 TRANSACTIONS OF THE GROTIUS SOCIETY 51 (1944), pp. 55–56; F.V. García Amador, Fourth Report of the Special Rapporteur, Responsibility of the State for Injuries Caused in its Territory to the Person or Property of Aliens—Measures Affecting Acquired Rights, 2 Y.B. Int'l L. Comm. 1 (United Nations 1959), ¶ 6; and Andrew Newcombe and Lluís Paradell, Law and Practice of Investment Treaties: Standards of Treatment 95 (Kluwer Law International 2009).

157 Gordon, K. and J. Pohl, *Investment Treaties over Time—Treaty Practice and Interpretation in a Changing World* 23 (OECD Publ'n, Working Paper No. 2, 2015); Michael Reisman & Mahnoush Arsanjani, *Interpreting Treaties for the Benefit of Third Parties: The "Salvors Doctrine" and the Use of Legislative History in Investment Treaties*, 104 AM. J. INT'L L. 597, 598–599 (2010) ("[P]rovisions [of the Vienna Convention] have become something of a clause de style in international judgments and arbitral awards: whether routinely and briefly referred to or solemnly reproduced verbatim, they are not always systematically applied ....").

interpretation such as *lex specialis*.[158] Although in the hierarchy of interpretive tools listed in the VCLT, Article 31, decisions of international courts are only secondary sources, investment arbitration tribunals generally heavily rely on the decisions of prior tribunals.[159] This practice, while commendable, and some have considered it to create a *jurisprudence constante*,[160] ultimately has not succeeded in creating a coherent jurisprudence, principally due to the fact that neither international law, nor BITs or the ICSID Convention contemplate a role for *stare decisis* principles as used in common law systems.[161] The result has been a somewhat fragmented jurisprudence on several issues, including application of the MFN clauses to matters of procedure,[162] application of the umbrella clauses, applicability of the standard of compensation for expropriation in treaties to unlawful expropriations and so forth.

Jurisdiction

The main basis for establishing jurisdiction is consent of the parties, which we discussed earlier. Further, in order for a foreign investor to bring a claim,

---

158 *See* CAMPBELL MCLACHLAN, LAURENCE SHORE & MATTHEW WEINIGER, INTERNATIONAL INVESTMENT ARBITRATION: SUBSTANTIVE PRINCIPLES, ¶ 3.73, at 68 (OXFORD UNIVERSITY PRESS, 2007). Other interpretative approaches proposed include Todd G. Weiler's historical approach. TODD WEILER, INTERPRETATION OF INTERNATIONAL INVESTMENT LAW 22 (2013).

159 Gabrielle Kaufmann-Kohler, *Arbitral Precedent: Dream, Necessity or Excuse?*, 23 ARB. INT'L 357, 357 & n.2 (2007); *see also* Jeffery P. Commission, *Precedent in Investment Treaty Arbitration: A Citation Analysis of a Developing Jurisprudence*, 24 J. INT'L ARB. 129 (2007) (providing a statistical analysis of the use of the precedent in international arbitration).

160 Ian Laird & Rebecca Askew, Finality Versus Consistency: Does Investor-State Arbitration Need an Appellate System, 7 J. APP. PRAC. & PROCESS 285, 301 (2005) ("Despite the lack of formal stare decisis, the system of soft precedent has actually resulted in consistency amongst the tribunal decisions."); *see also* Andrea K. Björklund, *Investment Treaty Arbitral Decisions as Jurisprudence Constante*, *in* INTERNATIONAL ECONOMIC LAW: THE STATE AND FUTURE OF THE DISCIPLINE 265 (Colin Picker, Isabella Bunn & Douglas Arner eds., 2008); FRÉDÉRIC G. SOURGENS, A NASCENT COMMON LAW 253 (Brill 2015).

161 IAN BROWNLIE, PRINCIPLES OF PUBLIC INTERNATIONAL LAW 37–38 (Brill 6th ed. 2003) ("It is true that the [ICJ] ... does not observe a doctrine of precedent, except perhaps on matters of procedure. But it strives to maintain judicial consistency."); *see also* LASSA OPPENHEIM, INTERNATIONAL LAW: A TREATISE 111 (4th Ed., 1926).

162 *Maffezini v. Spain*, ICSID Case No. ARB/97/7 (Jan. 25, 2000), 5 ICSID Rep. 396 (2002). *Cf.* Plama Consortium Ltd. v. Bulgaria, ICSID Case No. ARB/03/24 (Feb. 8, 2005). *But see* Scott Vesel, *Clearing A Path Through A Tangled Jurisprudence: Most-Favored-Nation Clauses and Dispute Settlement Provisions in Bilateral Investment Treaties*, 32 YALE J. INT'L L. 125, 127 (2007) (reconciling various views).

HISTORY, MODERN PRACTICE, AND FUTURE PROSPECTS 37

the investor must prove that (1) the investor has an investment within the BIT definitions and (2) the investor is also a qualified investor under the treaty's definition. If the claim is filed before ICSID, the investor must also satisfy the requirements of the ICSID Convention.

Notion of Investment

The definition of investment under modern BITs is very broad and includes a variety of economic activities including ownership of shares, tangible and intangible property rights and so forth. By contrast, the ICSID Convention does not define what an investment is.[163] Arbitral tribunals, however, following the *Salini v. Morocco* case generally look into several factors to see whether a particular economic activity would constitute an investment for the purposes of the ICSID Convention.[164] These include the: (1) contribution of money or assets; (2) duration over which the project was to be implemented; (3) participation in the risk of the transaction; and (4) contribution to the economic development of the host state. The last element, contribution to economic development, has raised debate. At least one case has been dismissed on that basis,[165] and States have argued in various cases that without such contribution, an ICSID tribunal would lack jurisdiction.[166] In *MHS v. Malaysia*, however, an annulment committee overturned an award dismissing a case for lack of jurisdiction on the ground that the contribution element was not a mandatory requirement.[167] More progressive was perhaps the decision of the tribunal in

---

163   Article 25 of ICSID limits the subject matter jurisdiction under the convention to "any legal disputes arising directly out of an investment." ICSID Convention, *supra* note 137, art. 25. The convention, however, is silent on the definition of investment. DUGAN ET AL., *supra* note 26, at 256.
164   *Salini Costruttori S.P.A. v. Morocco*, ICSID Case No. ARB/00/4, Decision on Jurisdiction, ¶ 52 (July 23, 2001), 42 I.L.M 609, 622 (2003).
165   Patrick Mitchell, Annulment Decision, ¶ 39.
166   *See, e.g., Philip Morris Brands Sàrl, Philip Morris Products S.A. and Abal Hermanos S.A. v. Oriental Republic of Uruguay*, ICSID Case No. ARB/10/7 (2016).
167   *Malaysian Historical Salvors v. Malaysia*, ICSID Case No. ARB/05/10, Decision on Application for Annulment, ¶ 78, 84, (Apr. 16, 2009); *see also Abal Hermanos S.A. v. Uruguay*, ICSID Case No. ARB/10/7, Decision on Jurisdiction, ¶ 206, (July 2, 2013), ("In the Tribunal's view, the four constitutive elements of the Salini list do not constitute jurisdictional requirements to the effect that the absence of one or the other of these elements would imply a lack of jurisdiction."); *see also* Borzu Sabahi & Kabir Duggal, *Philip Morris Brands Sarl v. Oriental Republic of Uruguay International Decisions*, 108 AM. J. INT'L L. 67 (2014).

Romak v. Uzbekistan where a tribunal held that the *Salini* criteria apply even in non-ICSID contexts.[168]

These developments, aimed at creating a so-called "objective" definition of investment together with other factors, have ultimately influenced treaty practice of some States. The U.S. Model BITs 2004 and later model's definition of investment provides that an investment "means every asset that an investor owns or controls, directly or indirectly, that has the characteristics of an investment, including such characteristics as the commitment of capital or other resources, the expectation of gain or profit, or the assumption of risk."[169]

Legality of Investments

It may seem axiomatic that for investments to enjoy the benefits of a treaty, they must first have been created in accordance with relevant domestic laws. Some investment treaties spell out this requirement[170] and arbitral tribunals

---

168 *Romak S.A. (Switzerland) v. The Republic of Uzbekistan*, UNCITRAL, PCA Case No. AA280, ¶ 207 (2009) ("The Arbitral Tribunal therefore considers that the term 'investments' under the BIT has an inherent meaning (irrespective of whether the investor resorts to ICSID or UNCITRAL arbitral proceedings) entailing a contribution that extends over a certain period of time and that involves some risk.").

169 *See also* US Model BIT 2004 art. 1; CA-EU CETA, *supra* note 116, art. X.3 ("Every kind of asset that an investor owns or controls, directly or indirectly, that has the characteristics of an investment, which includes a certain duration and other characteristics such as the commitment of capital or other resources, the expectation of gain or profit, or the assumption of risk."); see most recently TTP, Investment Chapter, art. 9.1.

170 *See, e.g.,* Agreement for the Reciprocal Protection of Investments signed between the Republic of El Salvador and the Kingdom of Spain, (14 February 1995) 1983 UNTS 349, entered into force 20 February 1996, (El Salvador-Spain BIT) Article 2.1 (stating that "[e]ach Contracting Party shall promote in its territory investments of investors of the other Contracting Party and shall accept them in accordance with its legislation."); Agreement between the Government of the Republic of Costa Rica and the Government of Canada for the Protection and Promotion of Investment (18 March 1998), entered into force 29 September 1999 (Costa Rica-Canada BIT) Article 1(h)ii (defining investor as "any enterprise as defined by paragraph (b) of this Article, incorporated or duly constituted in accordance with applicable laws of one Contracting Party"); Agreement between the Federal Republic of Germany and the Republic of the Philippines on the Promotion and Reciprocal Protection of Investments (April 18, 1997) entered into force 29 September 1999 (Germany-Philippines BIT) Article 2.1 ("Each Contracting State shall promote as far as possible investments in its territory by investors of the other Contracting State and admit such investments in accordance with its Constitution, laws and regulations as referred to in Article 1 paragraph 1. Such investments shall be accorded fair and equitable treatment.").

such as *Inceysa v. El Salvador*[171] relying on such clauses, have dismissed cases where foreign investors had circumvented the local laws. Related to that are implications of corruption and the applicability of doctrine of unclean hand[172] in investment treaty arbitration. As early as 2006, the *World Duty Free* tribunal[173] dismissed a claim against Kenya because the investor had bribed Government officials. In recent years, allegations of bribery and other illegal activities have emerged with more frequency in investment arbitration disputes requiring a more in-depth analysis of the implications of such acts in terms of State responsibility and whether they should always lead to the dismissal of the cases as most tribunals have done so far.[174] These cases are normally dismissed, even where the treaty is silent on the issue of legality.[175]

---

171 *Inceysa Vallisoletane, SL v El Salvador*, ICSID Case No ARB/03/26, IIC 134, Award (August 2, 2006). *See also* Alasdair Ross Anderson and Others v Costa Rica, ICSID Case No ARB(AF)/07/3, IIC 437, Award (May 10th, 2010).

172 *See generally* Aloysius Llamzon, Corruption in International Investment Arbitration (Oxford 2014); and Carolyn B. Lamm, Brody K. Greenwald, and Kristen M. Young, *From World Duty Free to Metal-Tech: A Review of International Investment Treaty Arbitration Cases Involving Allegations of Corruption*, 29(2) ICSID Review 328 (2014).

173 *World Duty Free Company Limited v. Republic of Kenya*, ICSID Case No. ARB/00/7, Award (October 2006).

174 Santiago Montt suggests that "treating domestic illegality as an issue of merits constitutes [...] a more balanced approach". *See* Santiago Montt, *supra* note 18, at 247.

175 *See e.g. Plama Consortium Limited v. Republic of Bulgaria*, ICSID Case No. ARB/03/24, IIC 338, Award, ¶ 138 (August 27th, 2008) (declaring the case inadmissible after noting that "[u]nlike a number of Bilateral Investment Treaties, the [Energy Charter Treaty/ECT] does not contain a provision requiring the conformity of the Investment with a particular law. This does not mean, however, that the protections provided for by the ECT cover all kinds of investments including those contrary to domestic or international law"; *Yukos Universal Limited (Isle of Man) v. The Russian Federation*, UNCITRAL, PCA Case No. AA 227, Final Award, ¶ 1349 (July 18th 2014) (noting *obiter dicta* that even where the applicable investment treaty does not contain an express requirement of compliance with host State laws (as is the case with the ECT), an investment that is made in breach of the laws of the host State may either: (a) not qualify as an investment, thus depriving the tribunal of jurisdiction; or (b) be refused the benefit of the substantive protections of the investment treaty"; *Phoenix Action, Ltd. v. The Czech Republic*, ICSID Case No. ARB/06/5 ¶ 101 (April 15th, 2009) (stating that "States cannot be deemed to offer access to the ICSID dispute settlement mechanism to investments not made in good faith [and that] this condition—the conformity of the establishment of the investment with the national laws—is implicit even when not expressly stated in the relevant BIT.").

Investors

The definition of investor in modern investment treaties as well as the ICSID Convention (Article 25) includes natural as well as legal persons including corporations, state-owned enterprises, sovereign wealth funds and even non-profit organizations.[176] A recurring issue during the past several years for host States has been the phenomenon of "treaty shopping" and "forum shopping" in which foreign investors establish corporations of convenience to meet the nationality requirement of various BITs (and ICSID Convention Article 25) in order to take advantage of the protections of a treaty.[177] A related issue is investors' use of various companies and individuals in the chain of ownership to bring multiple claims against the host State of the investment. Such practices have been characterized as abusive and, in some cases, arbitral tribunals have dismissed a case on these grounds.[178] It is not fully clear however in what situations such claims have to be dismissed. As seen in the *Phoenix v. Czech Republic* case, logic and principle of international law (*ratione temporis* limitations) seem to dictate that restructuring for the purpose of bringing claims that are foreseeable should be considered abusive and impressible.[179] But so far, no consistent practice has been developed on this issue. Modern treaties however contain denial of benefits clauses that would foreclose some abusive claims.[180]

---

176   See DUGAN ET AL., *supra* note 26, Ch. 12; *see also* MCLACHLAN ET AL. *supra* note 158.

177   Such claims among others would be limited by jurisdiction *ratione temporis* of a tribunal. See *Venezuela Holdings v. Venezuela*, ICSID Case No. ARB/07/27, Decision on jurisdiction (June 10, 2010) (investors established companies in a Dutch territory in order to bring claims against Venezuela under the Venezuela-Netherlands BIT). On parallel proceedings the classic cases are CME and Lauder cases against the Czech Republic. *See, e.g., Lauder v. Czech Republic*, 9 ICSID Rep. 62 (2001); CME v. Czech, 9 ICSID Rep. 340 (2001). Most recently see Lao Holdings and Sanum cases against the Lao People's Democratic Republic.

178   *Phoenix v. Czech Republic*, *supra* note 175, ¶ 32 (The tribunal held "that the whole 'investment' was an artificial transaction to gain access to ICSID." Id. ¶ 143.

179   Id.

180   US Model BIT 2012, *supra* note 9, Article 17.

   2. A Party may deny the benefits of this Treaty to an investor of the other Party that is an enterprise of such other Party and to investments of that investor if the enterprise has no substantial business activities in the territory of the other Party and persons of a non-Party, or of the denying Party, own or control the enterprise. *See also* the TPP, *supra* note 124, art. 9.15 (1).

State Defenses

Host states may raise various defenses to justify their failure to abide by their international obligations. These defenses are mainly derived from the Articles on State Responsibility of the International Law Commission's "circumstances precluding wrongfulness" which include: force major, distress and necessity.[181] Argentina particularly relied on the defense of necessity in the cases that were filed against it in the aftermath of the financial crisis of 2001–02.

Investment treaties may also contain provisions limiting State's responsibility in case of war, civil strife and other matters. Argentina invoked such provisions in the context of the same series of cases.

Counterclaims

In investment treaty arbitration there is limited opportunity for host States to bring counterclaims, even though, in theory, all arbitration rules allow counterclaims so long as the claim is within the scope of parties' consent to arbitration.[182] In fact, until the recent decisions in *Occidental Petroleum v. Ecuador*,[183] *Inmaris v. Ukraine*,[184] *Goetz v. Burundi*,[185] and *Urbaser v. Argentina* no arbitral tribunal had asserted jurisdiction over counterclaims. In *Goetz* [and *Inmaris*] the broad dispute resolution clause of the BIT, led the tribunal to infer that the disputing parties had consented to arbitrate the counterclaim.[186]

---

[181] See Draft Articles on Responsibility of States for Internationally Wrongful Acts, in Report of the International Law Commission on the Work of Its Fifty-third Session, UN GAOR, 56th Sess., Supp. No. 10, at 43, UN Doc. A/56/10 (2001) Articles 23, 24 & 25.

[182] ICSID Convention, *supra* note 137, art 40:

> (1) Except as the parties otherwise agree, a party may present an incidental or additional claim or counter-claim arising directly out of the subject-matter of the dispute, provided that such ancillary claim is within the scope of the consent of the parties and is otherwise within the jurisdiction of the Centre. *See also* 2010 UNCITRAL Rules, *supra* note 139, art. 22.

[183] *Occidental Petroleum Corp and Occidental Exploration and Production Company v Republic of Ecuador*, ICSID Case No. ARB/06/11, Award, ¶ 854–869 (Oct. 5th, 2012) (rejecting the counterclaim on the merits without discussing jurisdiction or admissibility).

[184] *Inmaris Perestroika Sailing Maritime Services GmbH and others v Ukraine*, ICSID Case No. ARB/08/8, Award (Mar. 1, 2012) (Inmaris v. Ukraine) (rejecting the counterclaim on the merits).

[185] *Antoine Goetz and others v Republic of Burundi*, ICSID Case No ARB/01/2, Award (June 21, 2012) (rejecting the counterclaim on the merits).

[186] Id. ¶ 277.

More recently, the counterclaims in *Burlington v. Ecuador*[187] and *Perenco v. Ecuador*[188] satisfied the requirement of consent as part of the jurisdictional inquiry. In *Burlington*, the parties' consent to the counterclaim was granted by a post-dispute agreement, while in *Perenco*, consent was implied from the broad language of the arbitration clause of the BIT.[189] However, investment treaties generally contain a narrow dispute resolution clause, which grants the investor the *exclusive* right to file international arbitration claims.[190] Only a handful of treaties explicitly recognize the right to counterclaim.[191] This asymmetry has been one of the reasons for the criticism of the modern investor-State arbitration according to critics of the system.

Compensation, Damages, and Valuation[192]

Assessment of damages is probably the most complex part of an international arbitration as it requires close coordination with, and input from, valuation and economic experts to quantify damages. As to the measure of compensation in expropriation cases, investment treaties generally require payment of fair market value (FMV), calculated immediately before expropriation.[193]

---

187 *Burlington Resources Inc. v. Republic of Ecuador*, ICSID Case No. ARB/08/5, Decision on Ecuador's Counterclaims (February 7th, 2017).

188 *Perenco Ecuador Ltd. v. The Republic of Ecuador and Empresa Estatal Petróleos del Ecuador (Petroecuador)*, ICSID Case No. ARB/08/6, Interim Decision on the Environmental Counterclaim, (August 11, 2015).

189 France-Ecuador Bilateral Investment Treaty, Article 9 paragraph 3 (1994) (recognizing the right to institute legal proceedings to either the foreign investor or the State arising out of a dispute). In *Burlington v Ecuador* and *Perenco v Ecuador*, the underlying contracts—which referred the disputing parties to initiate ICSID proceedings—were regarded as further evidence of consent to the ICSID counterclaim. The contracts contained the investor's obligations, and were connected to the subject matter of the primary claim.

190 *See e.g.* Energy Charter Treaty, *supra* note 101, Article 26 (2) (conferring the right to submit a claim to arbitration to the disputing investor only), CA-EU CETA, *supra* note 116, art. 8.23 (same), US Model BIT 2012, *supra* note 9, Article 1 & 24 (same).

191 *See e.g.* COMESA Investment Agreement, *supra* note 121, art. 28 (9), Southern African Development Community (SADC) Model BIT, Article 19 (2) (July 2012), Bilateral Investment Treaty between the Government of India and the Government of [Country] Model BIT, Article 14.11 (2016).

192 *See generally* Irmgard Marboe, CALCULATION OF COMPENSATION AND DAMAGES IN INTERNATIONAL INVESTMENT LAW (2nd ed. OUP Oxford, 2017); Sergey Ripinsky and Kevin Williams, DAMAGES IN INTERNATIONAL INVESTMENT LAW (BIILC, 2008); Borzu Sabahi, COMPENSATION AND RESTITUTION IN INVESTOR-STATE ARBITRATION: PRINCIPLES AND PRACTICE (OUP Oxford, 2011).

193 *See, e.g.*, NAFTA, *supra* note 96, art. 1110.

It is debated whether such standard applies to illegal expropriation (e.g., an expropriation not for a public purpose or that does not meet the other conditions of lawful expropriation). The *Chorzów Factory* case is the most relied upon case from which to derive the principle on reparation for wrongful expropriation and damages related to other BIT standards, such as FET and national treatment. The PCIJ held that "reparation must, as far as possible, wipe out all the consequences of the illegal act and reestablish the situation which would, in all probability, have existed if that act had not been committed."[194] In recent years, in the wake of nationalizations taking place in the hydrocarbons sector during a period of rising oil prices, a number of legal and valuation related questions have arisen and various tribunals are still grappling with these issues. Chief among them have been whether a mere non-payment of compensation is a ground for illegal expropriation. Moreover, as FMV might vary—through passage of time between the expropriation date and the date of calculation, or date of a hearing—the issue is whether subsequent events, such as the state of the market at the time of assesment, should be considered, and if so, to what extent. A related issue has been whether illegal expropriation would give a choice to the foreign investor to seek value of the property at the point in time when the property had the highest value. This is based on the assumption that "but for" the expropriation, the investor would sell the property at its peak price and various assumptions can be made in order to develop the "but for" scenario. The *Yukos Awards* of 2014[195] in which the tribunal ordered Russia to pay US$50 billion, as well as other "mega" cases[196] filed against Ecuador and Venezuela have highlighted the importance of clearer guidelines and methodologies for assessing damages. With respect to other treaty violations (e.g., FET and NT), principles of reparation derived from customary international law determine the amount of compensation due.

Annulment and Enforcement

Once an award is rendered, a losing party may seek to alter or overturn the award. Both the ICSID Convention, and the New York Convention (applicable in non-ICSID cases) have limited grounds for challenging arbitral awards, which focus principally on whether the arbitral process was conducted

---

194 Factory at Chorzów, Judgment 1928 P.C.I.J. (ser. A) No. 17 p. 47. (Sept. 13).

195 *Yukos Universal Limited (Isle of Man) v. The Russian Federation*, UNCITRAL, PCA Case No. AA 227, Award (18 July 2014).

196 George Kahale III coined the term "mega case" in 2014 to refer to multi-billion dollar claims against host Governments. See G. Kahale, III, Is Investor-State Arbitration Broken? TDM, October 2012, p. 8.

properly rather than on the substance.[197] The generally held view therefore is that mechanisms for annulment of investment treaty arbitration awards are not appeals. In exceptional circumstances, however, arbitration awards and commentators consider annulling an award for manifest errors of law which is not dissimilar to an appeal.[198]

VIII   Scaling Back Protections and Backlash

Thus far, it has been established that standards of investment protection have been widely accepted and incorporated into BITs and other international investment agreements, which have rapidly proliferated since the early 1990s. These substantive protections have been complemented by investor-State arbitration as the preferred method of dispute resolution over national litigation. However, this system of protection has often been criticized for a lack of legitimacy, and an inherent asymmetry that favors foreign investors.[199] Some critics have argued against the international investment system in the US and Europe, the former by questioning the economic benefits of NAFTA, and the latter by attempting to eliminate the system of investor-State arbitration in favor of a court-like model more like the WTO Dispute Settlement Body ("DSB").

A   *The EU Proposal of a European Investment Court System*

In response to these criticisms, a number of States have been re-assessing the costs and benefits of investor-State arbitration. The purported lack of impartiality of arbitrators, coupled with the absence of *stare decisis* has created, to an extent, distrust in investor-State Dispute Settlement (ISDS).[200] As a result, a small

---

197   Article 52 of the ICSID Convention, for example, lists five grounds: (a) that the Tribunal was not properly constituted; (b) that the Tribunal has manifestly exceeded its powers; (c) that there was corruption on the part of a member of the Tribunal; (d) that there has been a serious departure from a fundamental rule of procedure; or (e) that the award has failed to state the reasons on which it is based.

198   See most recently Occidental v. Ecuador (2015) (annulling a portion of the award in which the tribunal had mistakenly assumed the claimant owned 100 % of the expropriated concession rather than 60%, reducing damages awarded by more than US$ 700 million).

199   UNCTAD, *Reform of Investor-State Dispute Settlement in search of a roadmap*, Issue N. 3, at 10 (June 2013) *available at* http://heinonline.org/HOL/LandingPage?handle=hein.journals/mjiel10&div=28&id=&page=.

200   *See* Cecilia Malmström, "Proposing an Investment Court System" (16 September 2015), European Commission blog, *available at* <https://ec.europa.eu/commission/commissioners/2014-2019/malmstrom/blog/proposing-investment-court-system_en>.

number of states have eliminated ISDS from their investment agreements,[201] while others are making substantial revisions to their investment framework.[202] Europe, in particular, has been vocal against ISDS and has put forth their solution to the allegedly flawed system. In July 2015, the EU Commission made public a proposal for the creation of a Multilateral Permanent Investment Court. A few months later, the EU Parliament officially adopted the proposal. The goal of the EU is to create a standing investment court for each investment treaty it concludes. These courts will eventually merge and lead to the establishment of a multilateral investment court system.[203]

The EU initiative was officially presented to the US as part of their ongoing negotiations of the Transatlantic Trade and Investment Partnership ("TTIP"). Had the US adopted the EU's proposal for TTIP, the EU-US investment court would have consisted of a 'Tribunal of First Instance' (Tribunal) and an 'Appeal Tribunal'. The Tribunal would hear cases in divisions consisting of 3 judges appointed by the State parties only (and not investors), selected at random from a 15-judge roster developed by the EU and the US.[204] To ensure that each candidate is truly independent, a candidate would be scrutinized by the EU-US Joint Committee comprised of government representatives before inclusion in the roster.[205] These judges would be required to meet certain qualifications such as those required to sit as a judge in their home jurisdiction and demonstrated expertise in International Law.[206] The Tribunal hearing a case would be composed of a judge national of the EU, one of the US and one of a third country; all of whom would be selected at random to hear a case when a dispute arises.

---

201 UNCTAD, WORLD INVESTMENT REPORT-REFORMING INTERNATIONAL INVESTMENT GOVERNANCE, 152 (2015) (*hereinafter* UNCTAD 2015 Report) (indicating that "Australia–Japan Economic Partnership Agreement (EPA) (2014), the Australia–Malaysia FTA 2012, the Australia–New Zealand CEPA (2011), the Japan–Philippines EPA 2006, the Australia—United States FTA 2004, and the recently concluded CFIAs by Brazil with Angola and Mozambique [...] leave investment disputes subject to domestic courts but complement this process with the possibility of State-State proceedings under the treaty."

202 Id. (stating that "[at] least 50 countries or regions are currently revising or have recently revised their model IIAs.").

203 European Commission, *Transatlantic Trade and Investment Partnership: Trade in Services, Investment and E-Commerce* 17, Section 3—Resolution of Investment Disputes and Investment Court System, Article. Article 12 (2015) (hereinafter EU Commission Proposal, at http://trade.ec.europa.eu/doclib/docs/2015/september/tradoc_153807.pdf.)

204 Id. art. 9 (2).

205 Id. art. 11 paragraph 1.

206 Id. art. 9 paragraph 4.

To ensure legal consistency, a six-judge Appeal Tribunal would be established to hear appeals of the awards. The Appeal Tribunal would have jurisdiction to hear appeals based on legal errors, factual errors or any other challenge made under article 52 of the ICSID Convention, which provides grounds of the annulment of an award.[207] Currently, ICSID does not provide grounds for annulment on legal or factual errors making the European model an attractive alternative for critics who value correctness of awards.[208] The aim of the appeal system is to correct an award, in whole or in part, rather than annul it.[209] The final award would then be enforced under either the ICSID or the New York Convention.[210] The notion of an appeal body is not unique to the EU proposal. Several modern treaties, such as US—CAFTA-DR and the current US Model BIT, have provided for negotiations to be held to create an appellate mechanism to review awards (but no such bodies have been created as of the writing of this paper). One could speculate that the coexistence of EU investment tribunals alongside ad-hoc tribunals might lead to further fragmentation of international investment law. However, as the EU investment courts may eventually subsume into a single system, the ideas is that unity and coherence would be created for Europe and its partners.

The European proposal purports to introduces new and rigourous standards to secure the independence of judges, in response to this point of contention with ISDS. For example, a judge would not be allowed to act as counsel in any investment case while their tenure lasts to avoid the "double hat" issue.[211] In addition, judges would not be affiliated with any government, nor take instruction from them.[212] Even though arbitrators would not be explicitly prohibited from acting as expert witnesses, as stated in CETA,[213] the TTIP proposal reiterates that arbitrators must refrain from participating in any dispute that would create a direct or indirect conflict of interest.[214] The EU proposal, unlike the IBA

---

207 Id. art. 29 paragraph 1.
208 Eun Young Park, *Appellate Review in Investor-State Arbitration*, RESHAPING INVESTOR-STATE DISPUTE SETTLEMENT SYSTEM, JOURNEY FOR THE 21ST CENTURY, at 451 (Jean E Kalicki and Anna Joubin-Bret eds. 2015) (citing the drafting history of the ICSID Convention and indicating that "suggestions that a 'serious mistake in the application of the law' be included as ground of annulment were rejected because 'a mistake of the law as well as a mistake of fact constituted an inherent risk in judicial or arbitral decision'").
209 EU Commission Proposal, *supra* note 203, art. 29 paragraph 2.
210 Id. art. 6 paragraph 2.
211 Id. art. 11 paragraph 1.
212 Id.
213 CA-EU CETA, *supra* note 116, Article 8.30.
214 EU Commission Proposal, *supra* note 203, Article 11 paragraph 1.

guidelines, provides discretionary grounds for disclosure,[215] and obliges judges to disclose any circumstances or facts that might affect their independence or create an appearance of bias in the proceeding.[216] Challenges to members of the Tribunal or Appeal Tribunal are decided by the President of the respective tribunal.[217] This does not improve upon the current method by which ICSID in particular evaluates arbitrator challenges. Conversely, the EU-Canada trade deal, CETA, which establishes the EU's first bilateral investment court, contains a code of a conduct but leaves the decision on a conflict of interest to an external actor, the President of the International Court of Justice.[218]

Will the European Court System be Better than the Current System of ISDS?

The establishment of the European investment court system under TTIP or CETA poses a number of important legal and political issues. The proposal does not provide a mechanism by which 28 European states will agree upon a short list of 5 EU judges for inclusion in the roster. Every state may want to be represented because these judges could act in potential cases brought against them. In contrast, the US or Canada would be represented by its own judge in any potential dispute with an EU counterparty. Despite the procedures implemented to ensure independence, it remains to be seen if the European model will indeed guarantee such independence. Judges will be entirely elected and re-elected by states, creating an appearance of bias towards them. This model might generate a situation of benevolence towards the state since judges are elected for a 6 year term, with a possible 6 year renewal at the hand of the appointing state(s). It can be argued that this method of election does not depart from the "party appointed arbitrator" system that ISDS has been criticized for. Additionally, as explained earlier, the current system of investment protection already provides mechanisms for dealing with the alleged lack of impartiality, and has the potential to be strengthened.

Moreover, and although the model seeks jurists with recognized competence in international law, it makes expertise in international investment law *desirable*.[219] While international law plays an important role in international investment arbitration, as the former interacts and complements the latter, international investment law has evolved and operates as *lex specialis*. Thus,

---

215 2014 IBA Guidelines, *supra* note 138, Part II (6).
216 EU Commission Proposal, *supra* note 203, Annex II, art. 3.
217 Id. Article 11.3.
218 CA-EU CETA, *supra* note 116, Article 8.30.3.
219 EU Commission Proposal, *supra* note 203, Article 9 paragraph 4.

it would seem that the proposal diminishes the fact that international investment law has emerged as a specialized field, with its own rules and practices.

Some have additionally argued that the issue of inconsistent rulings in ISDS will not be eliminated with the creation of a court system. In support of this argument, it has been noted that international investment law itself is not well settled,[220] as it is a relatively young field of international law.[221] Along the same lines, as there are over 3000 investment treaties, each with different investment standards, the court system will be unable to achieve the consistency promised (in contrast to the WTO DSB, which operates under a single treaty).

Despite these critiques, Europe has taken strong steps to institute its alternative to ISDS by introducing the establishment of a multilateral court system. With CETA entering into force provisionally, the establishment of the first standing investment court will guide the development of any future courts.[222] Following CETA, the EU-Vietnam FTA provides for the creation of a similar investment court, which will further test the EUs alternative to ISDS.[223] The court model is also part of the ongoing negotiations of FTAs between the EU and Mexico,[224] Singapore, and Japan.[225] It remains to be seen if the US will acquiesce to Europe's investment court model as the US has never lost an ISDS case and its model BIT, which provides for the establishment of ad-hoc arbitral tribunals, has been widely accepted by its trading partners.

The fate of TTIP is currently on hold, despite seeking to increase trade and investment opportunities between the US and the EU.[226] While the TTIP

---

220   Luis Gonzalez Garcia, *Making Impossible Investor-State Reform Possible*, in RESHAPING INVESTOR-STATE DISPUTE SETTLEMENT SYSTEM, JOURNEY FOR THE 21ST CENTURY, *supra* note 208, at 432.

221   Gabriel Bottini, *Reform of the Investor-State Arbitration Regime: The Appeal Proposal*, in RESHAPING INVESTOR-STATE DISPUTE SETTLEMENT SYSTEM, JOURNEY FOR THE 21ST CENTURY, *supra* note 208, at 465 (citing LM. Ten Cate).

222   CA-EU CETA, *supra* note 116.

223   *See* EU—Vietnam Free Trade Agreement (2 December 2015) pending entering into force, available at <http://trade.ec.europa.eu/doclib/press/index.cfm?id=1437> (last visited September 25, 2017).

224   *See* EU—Mexico Free Trade Agreement, EU Textual Proposal on Investment and Trade in Services, Chapter I, section C "Resolution of Investment Disputes and Investment Court System" (as of April 2017), *available at.* <http://trade.ec.europa.eu/doclib/docs/2017/may/tradoc_155521.pdf> (last visited Ocotber 1, 2017).

225   European Commission, *Overview of FTA and other Trade Negotiations* (updated September 2017), *available at* <http://trade.ec.europa.eu/doclib/docs/2006/december/tradoc_118238.pdf > (last visited October 3, 2017).

226   The EU is the largest regional investor and trading partner of the United States. For further reference *see* Organization for International Investment, *Foreign Direct Investment in*

negotiations were suspended, the US has formally decided not to join the Trans-Pacific Partnership Agreement (TPP),[227] a decision that became effective in January 2017. The Trump administration's decision was based on a concern for the TPP's potentially devastating impact on the American economy by further injuring the domestic manufacturing and labour markets. For the same reason, the US has proposed major revisions of the NAFTA agreement.

B *The US Proposal for a Revised NAFTA*

The NAFTA partners have started the process of revising the 23-year-old trade agreement. One goal is to include into NAFTA the legal evolutions, innovations and trends of the new generation of free trade agreements. These agreements cover a broader range of topics, are more indepth and seek to secure the right of the host state to regulate in the public interest. In July 2017, the US Trade Representative (USTR) made public the goals the US would seek to achieve in renegotiating NAFTA.[228] As renegotiations are ongoing at the time of this writing, the examination of key issues in NAFTA renegotiations is based on the goals officially announced by the USTR.

The US seeks to transform NAFTA into an engine of economic growth, and modernize NAFTA to meet the business practices of the 21st Century. The latter includes the incorporation of a chapter on digital trade and e-commerce, which were nonexistent in the early 1990s.[229] The renegotiation also aims at introducing a prohibition against currency manipulation, which grants governments an unfair competitive trade advantage.[230] While neither Mexico nor

---

the *United States 2017 Report*, at 4 (stating that "[Europe] made up 60 percent of all foreign investment through 2016"), *available at* http://ofii.org/sites/default/files/FDIUS%202017.pdf. (last visited August 28, 2017). *See also* US Department of Commerce, *U.S. Commerce Department Releases New Report on Foreign Direct Investment Trends* (20 June 2016) (stating that "The largest sources of FDI into the United States are advanced economies, led by the United Kingdom, Japan, and Germany."), *available at* <https://www.commerce.gov/news/press-releases/2016/06/us-commerce-department-releases-new-report-foreign-direct-investment> (last visited October 15, 2017).

227 For further reference *see* the Trans-Pacific Partnership Agreement (TPP) Chapter 9 Section B (February 4th, 2016) pending entering into force, *available at* <https://ustr.gov/trade-agreements/free-trade-agreements/trans-pacific-partnership/tpp-full-text>.

228 Office of the United States Trade representatives, Executive Office of the President, Summary of Objectives for the NAFTA Renegotiation (July 17th, 2017) (hereinafter USTR Nafta Renegotiation Objectives) *available at.* <https://ustr.gov/sites/default/files/files/Press/Releases/NAFTAObjectives.pdf> Last visited August 25, 2017.

229 Id. at 8.

230 Id. at 17.

Canada have a history of currency manipulation, the US is seeking to introduce this prohibition in an effort to standardize its relationship with its trading partners. Further, the US aims to formalize labor and environmental provisions in NAFTA, integrating and deepening the commitments made in the earlier side agreements.[231] The NAFTA parties, in the course of negotiating the environmental and labor standards of the TPP, reached a consensus on key standards, which should be easily incorporated into NAFTA.[232]

There remains, however, other challenging and contentious issues for the parties to agree upon. First, the US's main goal is to reverse its persistent trade in goods deficit within NAFTA. In order to reverse this deficit, the US is seeking to increase market access opportunities for exports of U.S. products to Mexico and Canada.[233] Several strategies will be proposed to achieve this goal, however, it is uncertain whether Canada and Mexico will accept an increase in US exports. Among such initiatives is the US proposal to amend the NAFTA Rules of Origin by requiring higher NAFTA content, and substantial US content.[234] Second, the US is proposing to eliminate the NAFTA bi-national panel, which reviews antidumping (AD) and countervailing duties (CVD) issued by competent national authorities.[235] The goal of the US is to empower domestic courts to make final determinations of AD and CVD, and to "[p]reserve the ability of the US to enforce rigorously its trade laws".[236] It seems unlikely that Canada and Mexico would agree to expose their exporters to challenge AD and CVD decisions in US courts as it would arguably leave exporters without any impartial recourse. Third, as negotiations have become more complex, it has been revealed that the US is seeking to introduce a "sunset clause" according to which NAFTA would terminate every 5 years, unless the parties agree to renew it.[237] This clause would create uncertainty in the business environment as investors would not be given assurances that they will recieve investment protections beyond a five-year term.

---

231 Id. at 12–13.
232 See TPP, *supra* note 124, Chapters 18 and 19.
233 USTR Nafta Renegotiation Objectives, *supra* note 228, at 4.
234 Id. at 6. This debate is currently focusing on the automotive industry. At present, the NAFTA value content for autos is 62.5% and it is presumed that any increase may make NAFTA-made vehicles less competitive especially in the NAFTA market.
235 Id. at 14–15.
236 Id.
237 Ana Swanson, *How the Trump Administration Is Doing Renegotiating Nafta*, The New York Times, (September 28, 2017) *available at* <https://www.nytimes.com/2017/09/28/business/how-the-trump-administration-is-doing-renegotiating-nafta.html> (last visited Oct 7, 2017).

Canada's trade agreement with the European Union, CETA, has the potential to influence ongoing NAFTA re-negotiations. In particular, the right to regulate in the public interest has been challenged by investors under NAFTA. Canada has responded to this aspect in CETA by explicitly granting governments strong regulatory powers to protect the public interest.[238] CETA'S FET clause further defines in detail the particular grounds giving rise to FET violation, so as to remove any attempt to challenge the government's regulatory actions.[239] This developed FET clause is an aspect Canada may seek to propose to achieve consistency in its domestic regulatory policy in the context of the NAFTA renegotiations.

Following the trend of modern BITs, CETA and the TPP have incorporated provisions to combat corruption, which NAFTA currently lacks. CETA provides that an investor that makes an investment by means of "fraudulent misrepresentation, concealment, corruption, or conduct amounting to an abuse of process" loses the right to bring an investor-State claim.[240] The TPP contains strong provisions mandating the parties to combat and punish corruption and bribes given to public officials "affecting trade and investment".[241] The incorporation of strong anti-corruption provisions in NAFTA will increase adherence to the rule of law and encourage healthy government procurement practices.

But, perhaps, government procurement renegotiations might become one of the most contentious aspects of the NAFTA negotiations. The US seeks to increase access to the Mexican and Canadian government procurement markets. It however intends to restrict Canadian and Mexican companies from participating in state and local tendering procedures,[242] because it has implemented a "Buy America" policy for state and local projects.[243] This posture conflicts with Canada's position on government procurement, as indicated in CETA,

---

238 See CA-EU CETA, supra note 116, art. 8.9.

  1. For the purpose of this Chapter, the Parties reaffirm their right to regulate within their territories to achieve legitimate policy objectives, such as the protection of public health, safety, the environment or public morals, social or consumer protection or the promotion and protection of cultural diversity.

  2. For greater certainty, the mere fact that a Party regulates, including through a modification to its laws, in a manner which negatively affects an investment or interferes with an investor's expectations, including its expectations of profits, does not amount to a breach of an obligation under this Section."

239 See supra note 130.
240 See CA-EU CETA, supra note 116, art. 8.18.3.
241 See TPP, supra note 124, Article 26.7.
242 USTR Nafta Renegotiation Objectives, supra note 228, at 15–16.
243 Id. at 16.

which liberalizes access to public procurement markets at all levels of government, in all sectors in Canada with respect to EU suppliers.[244] The US position will prevent it from reaching Canadian and Mexican provincial, state and local governmental projects, because access is granted on reciprocal grounds. Additionally, as the renegotiation progresses it will have to be seen whether NAFTA incorporates provisions on the protection of sustainable development, the rights of indigenous peoples and gender equality, all to which Canada affords strong protections.

The future of NAFTA is uncertain at the time of this writing. After more than 2 decades of free trade and investment, the economies of the NAFTA parties have become so closely linked that the chances of terminating NAFTA are low, yet possible. If no progress is achieved, the Trump administration has stated that the US will withdraw from NAFTA.[245] It is greatly speculated that should this happen, two separate trade agreements, with Mexico and Canada, would be concluded as a replacement and reshape the economies of North America.

IX   Conclusion

From the time of proliferation of treaties, the international community has entered into an "era of reorientation" of international investment law.[246] This is evidenced by the number of States that have begun revisions of BITs, some, more radically, by questioning the legitimacy of ISDS as a whole.[247] Together with the reorientation of ISDS, participation in mega trade blocs—such as CETA, TPP, TTIP and TISA,[248]—has become the preferred method for facilitating foreign investment. Mega blocs allow for countries to expeditiously engage with many new markets and to design an investment framework for an entire region. It has been emphasized that participation in "regional and, even more so, mega regional [blocs] offer opportunities to consolidate today's

---

244   CA-EU CETA, *supra* note 116, Chapter 19 and annexes.
245   Ashley Parker ET AL., *I was all set to terminate': Inside Trump's sudden shift on NAFTA*, THE WASHINGTON POST, April 27, 2017 *available at* <https://www.washingtonpost.com/politics/i-was-all-set-to-terminate-inside-trumps-sudden-shift-on-nafta/2017/04/27/0452a3fa-2b65-11e7-b605-33413c691853_story.html?utm_term=.d46ob112fef6>.
246   UNCTAD 2015, *supra* note 201, at 124.
247   *See supra* note 130.
248   Trade in Services Agreement (TiSA) composed of 23 WTO members, including the US and all EU member states, is currently under negotiations. For further reference *see* https://ustr.gov/TiSA (last visited October 3, 2017).

multifaceted and multi layered treaty network".[249] Particiaption in these blocs give states the opporutnity to strengthen and contribute to the emergence of new investment standards.[250]

For this reason, withdrawal from the TPP deprived the US of the opportunity to exert influence in the Asia-Pacific region. While participation in mega blocs is on the rise, the US's strong preference for bilateral negotiations is unchanged. On the other hand, a new mega trade bloc is emerging for Asia and trading partners. The Regional Comprehensive Economic Partnership (RCEP) is in process of formation and its most active negotiating members include China and India.[251] RCEP is expected to represent a major source of intra-regional trade and investment opportunities in Asia. While the terms of RCEP are currently under negotiation, it is uncertain whether RCEP and the new generation FTAs will contain similar or divergent investment standards. This uncertainty is due to China's influence particularly on issues such as labor, environment and intellectual property rights. However, over time, increased participation in mega trading blocs will facilitate more consistent investment standards for a region. Thus, RCEP might contribute to the process of gradual liberalization so as to construct a harmonious global system of investment protection.

Bibliography

Alvarez, Jose Enrique, The Public International Law Regime Governing International Investment, 344 Collected Courses of the Hague Academy of International Law 193, (2009).

AMERASINGHE, CHITTHARANJAN FELIX, LOCAL REMEDIES IN INTERNATIONAL LAW (2nd ed. 2004).

Bergsten, Eric, Americanization of International Arbitration, 18 PACE INT'L L. REV. 289, (2006).

Bernasconi-Osterwalder, Nathalie, The Draft Investment Chapter of the Canada-EU Comprehensive Economic and Trade Agreement: A Step Backwards for the EU and Canada?, INVESTMENT TREATY NEWS (June 26, 2013).

---

249   UNCTAD 2015, *supra* note 201, at 125.
250   Id. 125.
251   RCEP members are: Brunei, Cambodia, Indonesia, Laos, Malaysia, Myanmar, the Philippines, Singapore, Thailand, Vietnam, Australia, China, India, Japan, South Korea and New Zealand. For more information see http://asean.org/?static_post=rcep-regional-comprehensive-economic-partnership.

Bierbrauer, Elfriede, Negotiations on the EU-Canada Comprehensive Economic and Trade Agreement (CETA) Concluded, Directorate-Gen. for External Policies, European Parliament, (2014).

Birch, Nicholas J., Laird, Ian, Sabahi, Borzu, International Investment Law Regime and the Rule of Law as a Precondition for International Development, in New Directions in International Economic Law (Todd Weiler & Freya Baetens eds., 2011).

Bishop, R. Doak & Reed, Lucy, Practical Guidelines for Interviewing, Selecting and Challenging Party-Appointed Arbitrators in International Commercial Arbitration, 14 Arb. Int'l 2 (1998).

Björklund, Andrea K., Investment Treaty Arbitral Decisions as Jurisprudence Constante, in International Economic Law: The State and Future of the Discipline (Colin Picker, Isabella Bunn & Douglas Arner eds., 2008).

Borchard, Edwin, the Diplomatic Protection of Citizens Abroad (1915).

Borchard, Edwin, Minimum Standard of Treatment of Aliens, (1939) 33 ASIL Proc. 51.

Bottini, Gabriel, Reform of the Investor-State Arbitration Regime: The Appeal Proposal, Reshaping Investor-State Dispute Settlement System, Journey for the 21st Century (Jean E Kalicki and Anna Joubin-Bret eds. 2015).

Broches, Aron, Development of International Law by the International Bank for Reconstruction and Development, in Proceedings of ASIL 33, 81 (1965).

Brown, Chester, Introduction: The Development and Importance of the Model Bilateral Investment Treaty, in Commentaries on Selected Model Investment Treaties (Chester Brown ed., 2013).

Brownlie, Ian, Principles of Public International Law (6th ed. 2003).

Busse, Matthias, Königer, Jens and Nunnenkamp, Peter, FDI promotion through bilateral investment treaties: more than a bit?, Review of World Economics / Weltwirtschaftliches Archiv, Vol. 146, No. 1 (April 2010).

Cheng, Tai-Heng, Positivism, New Haven Jurisprudence, and the Fragmentation of International Law, in New Directions in International Economic Law (Todd Weiler & Freya Baetens eds., 2011).

Commission, Jeffery P., Precedent in Investment Treaty Arbitration: A Citation Analysis of a Developing Jurisprudence, 24 J. Int'l Arb. 129 (2007).

Crawford, James, Brownlie's Principles of Public International Law (8th ed. 2012).

Cremades, Bernardo M., Disputes Arising Out of Foreign Direct Investment in Latin America: A New Look at the Calvo Doctrine and Other Jurisdictional Issues, 59 Disp. Res. J. 78 (2004).

De Mestral, Armand, Pre-Entry Obligations under International Law, in International Investment Law (Bungenberg, Griebel, Hobe, Reinisch eds., CH Beck Hart Nomos 2015).

De Mestral, Armand, When Does the Exception Become the Rule? Conserving Regulatory Space under CETA, 18 J. INT'L ECON. L. 641, 643 (2015).

Dolzer, Rudolf & Schreuer, Christoph, Principles of International Investment Law (2nd ed., 2012).

Dolzer, Rudolf & Stevens, Margrete, Bilateral Investment Treaties 50 (1995).

Douglas, Zachary, The Hybrid Foundations of Investment Treaty Arbitration, 74 BRIT. Y.B. INT'L L. 151, (2003).

DUGAN, CHRISTOPHER F., WALLACE, DON, RUBINS, NOAH & SABAHI, BORZU, INVESTOR-STATE ARBITRATION (Oxford UP 2008).

Elkins, Zachary et al., Competing for Capital: The Diffusion of Bilateral Investment Treaties, 1960–2000, 2008 U. ILL. L. REV. 265 (2008).

Fitch, Stephen D., The Harriman Manganese Concession in the Soviet Union: Lessons for Today, 9 INT'L TAX & BUS. L. 209 (1991).

García Amador, F.V., Fourth Report of the Special Rapporteur, Responsibility of the State for Injuries Caused in its Territory to the Person or Property of Aliens—Measures Affecting Acquired Rights, 2 Y.B. Int'l L. Comm. 1 (United Nations 1959).

Gardner, John, Legal Positivism: 5 ½ Myths, 46 AM J. OF JURIS. 199 (2001).

Giorgetti, Chiara, Between Legitimacy and Control: Challenges and Recusals of Judges and Arbitrators in International Courts and Tribunals, 49 Geo. Wash. Int'l L. Rev. 205 (2017).

Goebel, Julius Jr., The International Responsibility of States for Injuries Sustained by Aliens on Account of Mob Violence, Insurrections and Civil Wars, 8 AM. J. INT'L L. 802 (1914).

Gómez-Palacio, Ignacio & Muchlinski, Peter, Admission and Establishment, in THE OXFORD HANDBOOK ON INTERNATIONAL INVESTMENT LAW (Peter Muchlinski, Federico Ortino, & Christoph Schreuer eds., 2008).

Gonzalez Garcia, Luis, Making Impossible Investor-State Reform Possible, RESHAPING INVESTOR-STATE DISPUTE SETTLEMENT SYSTEM, JOURNEY FOR THE 21ST CENTURY (Jean E Kalicki and Anna Joubin-Bret eds. 2015).

Gordon, K. & Pohl, J., Investment Treaties over Time—Treaty Practice and Interpretation in a Changing World (OECD Publ'n, Working Paper No. 2, 2015).

Grierson-Weiler, Todd J. & Laird, Ian A., Standards of Treatments, in THE OXFORD HANDBOOK, in THE OXFORD HANDBOOK ON INTERNATIONAL INVESTMENT LAW (Peter Muchlinski, Federico Ortino, & Christoph Schreuer eds., 2008).

Gudgeon, K., United States Bilateral Investment Treaties: Comments on Their Origin, Purposes, and General Treatment Standards, 4 INT'L TAX & BUS. L. 105 (1986).

Gus Van, Harten, The Public-Private Distinction in the International Arbitration of Individual Claims Against the State, 56 International & Comparative Law Quarterly (ICLQ) 371 (2007).

Hackworth, Green H., 3 Digest of International Law 655 (1942).
Harvard Law School Research in International Law, The Law of Responsibility of States for Damage Done in Their Territory to the Person or Property of Foreigners, 23 Am. J. Int'l L., Special Supp. 131 (1929).
Hawkins, Harry C., Commercial Treaties and Agreements: Principles and Practice (New York: Rinehart & Company Inc., 1951).
Houde, Marie-France & Yannaca-Small, K. Relationships between International Investment Agreements (OECD Publ'n Working Paper No. 1, 2004).
Houde, Marie-France, Novel Features in Recent OECD Bilateral Investment Treaties, in International Investment Perspectives (2006).
Jackson, John H., Davey, William J. & Sykes, Alan O., Legal Problems of International Economic Relations (4th ed. 2001).
Kahale, III, George, Is Investor-State Arbitration Broken? TDM, October 2012.
Kahn, Philip and Wälde, Thomas, Report for the Hague Academy 2004 in connection with the program "New Aspects of International Investment Law / Les aspects nouveaux du droit des investissements internationaux" (Ph. Kahn and T. W. Wälde eds., 2004).
Kaufmann-Kohler, Gabrielle, Arbitral Precedent: Dream, Necessity or Excuse?, 23 Arb. Int'l 357 (2007).
Kingsbury, Benedict & Schill, Stephan, Investor-State Arbitration as Governance: Fair and Equitable Treatment, Proportionality and the Emerging Global Administrative Law (September 2, 2009), NYU School of Law, Public Law Research Paper No. 09-46.
Kjos, Hege Elisabeth, Applicable Law in Investor-State Arbitration: The Interplay between National and International Law (Oxford University Press, 2013).
Kurtz, Jurgen, A General Investment Agreement in the WTO—Lessons from Chapter 11 of NAFTA and the OECD Multilateral Agreement on Investment, 23 U. Pa. J. Int'l L. 756 (2002).
Laird, Ian & Askew, Rebecca, Finality Versus Consistency: Does Investor-State Arbitration Need an Appellate System, 7 J. App. Prac. & Process 285 (2005).
Lamm, Carolyn B., Greenwald, Brody K., and Young, Kristen M., From World Duty Free to Metal-Tech: A Review of International Investment Treaty Arbitration Cases Involving Allegations of Corruption, 29(2) ICSID Review 328 (2014).
Lipstein, K., Conflict of Laws before International Tribunals, 29 Transactions of the Grotius Society 51 (1944).
Llamzon, Aloysius, Corruption in International Investment Arbitration (Oxford 2014).
Lowenfeld, Adreas F., International Economic Law (2nd ed. 2008).
Mackaay, Ejan History of Law and Economics, in 1 Encyclopedia of Law and Economics 65 (Boudewijn Bouckaert & Gerrit De Geest eds., 2000).

Manning-Cabrol, Denise, The Imminent Death of the Calvo Clause and the Rebirth of the Calvo Principle: Equality of Foreign and National Investors, 26 LAW & POL'Y INT'L BUS. 1169 (1995).

Marboe, Irmgard CALCULATION OF COMPENSATION AND DAMAGES IN INTERNATIONAL INVESTMENT LAW (OUP Oxford, 2009).

McLachlan, Campbell, Shore, Laurence & Weiniger, Matthew, INTERNATIONAL INVESTMENT ARBITRATION: SUBSTANTIVE PRINCIPLES (OXFORD UNIVERSITY PRESS, 2007).

MITCHELL, NANCY, THE DANGER OF DREAMS: GERMAN AND AMERICAN IMPERIALISM IN LATIN AMERICA (University of North Carolina Press, 1999).

Monagas, Yessika, U.S. Property in Jeopardy: Latin American Expropriations of U.S. Corporations' Property Abroad, 34 HOUS. J. INT'L L. 455 (2012).

Montt, Santiago, State Liability in Investment Treaty Arbitration: Global Constitutional Law and Administrative Law In The BIT Generation (2009).

NAFZIGER, WAYNE E., THE ECONOMICS OF DEVELOPING COUNTRIES (3rd ed. 1997).

Newcombe, Andrew and Paradell, Lluís, Law and Practice of Investment Treaties: Standards of Treatment (Kluwer Law International 2009).

Nussbaum, Arthur, Arbitration Between the Lena Goldfields Ltd. and the Soviet Government, 36 CORNELL L. REV. 31 (1950).

OPPENHEIM, LASSA, INTERNATIONAL LAW: A TREATISE 111 (4th Ed., 1926).

PARLETT, KATE, THE INDIVIDUAL IN THE INTERNATIONAL LEGAL SYSTEM: CONTINUITY AND CHANGE IN INTERNATIONAL LAW (Cambridge: Cambridge University Press, 2011).

Park, Eun Young, Appellate Review in Investor-State Arbitration, RESHAPING INVESTOR-STATE DISPUTE SETTLEMENT SYSTEM, JOURNEY FOR THE 21ST CENTURY (Jean E Kalicki and Anna Joubin-Bret eds. 2015).

Parra, Antonio, The History of ICSID (Oxford 2012).

Paulsson, Jan, Arbitration without Privity, ICSID Review (1995).

Paulsson, Jan, Moral Hazard in International Dispute Resolution, TDM, June 10, 2010.

Pauwelyn, Joost, At the Edge of Chaos? Foreign Investment Law as a Complex Adaptive System, How It Emerged and How It Can Be Reformed, 29 ICSID REV. 372 (2014).

RALSTON, JACKSON HARVEY, THE LAW AND PROCEDURE OF TRIBUNALS BEING A RÉSUMÉ OF THE VIEWS OF ARBITRATORS QUESTIONS ARISING UNDER THE LAW OF NATIONS (Stanford University Press rev. ed. 1926).

Reisman, Michael W., The View from the New Haven School of International Law, AMERICAN SOCIETY OF INTERNATIONAL LAW, PROCEEDINGS OF THE ANNUAL MEETING 118 (1992).

Reinisch, August, & Malintoppi, Loretta, Methods of Dispute Resolution, in THE OXFORD HANDBOOK ON INTERNATIONAL INVESTMENT LAW (Peter Muchlinski, Federico Ortino, & Christoph Schreuer eds., 2008).

Reisman, Michael, & Arsanjani, Mahnoush, Interpreting Treaties for the Benefit of Third Parties: The "Salvors Doctrine" and the Use of Legislative History in Investment Treaties, 104 AM. J. INT'L L. 597 (2010).

Ripinsky, Sergey and Williams, Kevin DAMAGES IN INTERNATIONAL INVESTMENT LAW (BIILC, 2008).

Roberts, Anthea, Clash of Paradigms: Actors and Analogies Shaping the Investment Treaty System, 107 AM. J. INT'L L. 45 (2013).

Root, Elihu, The Basis of Protection to Citizens Residing Abroad, 4 AM. J. INT'L L. 517 (1910).

Roth, Andreas H., The minimum standard of international law applied to aliens (Leiden: A.W. Sijthoff, 1949).

Sabahi, Borzu, COMPENSATION AND RESTITUTION IN INVESTOR-STATE ARBITRATION: PRINCIPLES AND PRACTICE (OUP Oxford, 2011).

Sabahi, Borzu & Duggal, Kabir, Philip Morris Brands Sarl v. Oriental Republic of Uruguay International Decisions, 108 AM. J. INT'L L. 67 (2014).

Schill, Stephan W., The Multilateralization of International Investment Law (Cambridge University Press, 2009).

Schreuer, Christoph, Consent to Arbitration, in THE OXFORD HANDBOOK, in THE OXFORD HANDBOOK ON INTERNATIONAL INVESTMENT LAW (Peter Muchlinski, Federico Ortino, & Christoph Schreuer eds., 2008).

Schreuer, Christoph, Malintoppi, Loretta, Reinisch, August, and Sinclair, Anthony, The ICSID Convention: A Commentary (2nd ed., Cambridge, 2009).

Schwarzenberger, Georg, The Abs-Shawcross Draft Convention on Investments Abroad: A Critical Commentary, 9 J. PUB. L. 147 (1960).

SHIHATA, IBRAHIM F. I. MIGA AND FOREIGN INVESTMENT (1988).

Sikkink, Kathryn, Reconceptualizing Sovereignty in the Americas: Historical Precursors and Current Practices, 19 HOUS. J. INT'L L. 705 (1997).

Simma, Bruno & Paulus, Andreas L., Symposium on Method in International Law: The Responsibility of Individuals for Human Rights Abuses in Internal Conflicts: A Positivist View, 93 AM. J. INT'L L. 302 (1999).

Skovgaard Poulsen, Lauge N., book review [Karl P. Sauvant, and Lisa E. Sachs. (eds). The Effect of Treaties on Foreign Direct Investment: Bilateral Investment Treaties, Double Taxation Treaties, and Investment Flows.] Eur J Int Law (2009).

Sloss, David, The Domestication of International Human Rights: Non-Self-Executing Declarations and Human Rights Treaties, 24 Yale J. Int'l L. 129 (1999).

SORNARAJAH, M., RESISTANCE AND CHANGE IN THE INTERNATIONAL LAW OF FOREIGN INVESTMENT (2015).

SOURGENS, FRÉDÉRIC G. A NASCENT COMMON LAW (Brill | Nijhoff, 2015).

Spiegel, Hans W., Origin and Development of Denial of Justice, 32 AM. J. INT'L L. 63 (1938).

Steingruber, Andrea Marco, Consent in International Arbitration (Oxford 2012).

UNCTAD, National Treatment, in UNCTAD SERIES ON ISSUES IN INTERNATIONAL INVESTMENT AGREEMENTS II (1999).

UNCTAD, WORLD INVESTMENT REPORT—FOREIGN DIRECT INVESTMENT AND THE CHALLENGE OF DEVELOPMENT (1999).

UNCTAD, Admission and Establishment, in UNCTAD SERIES ON ISSUES IN INTERNATIONAL INVESTMENT AGREEMENTS (2002).

UNCTAD, Most-Favoured Nation Treatment, in UNCTAD SERIES ON ISSUES IN INTERNATIONAL INVESTMENT AGREEMENTS II (2010).

UNCTAD, Fair and Equitable Treatment, in UNCTAD SERIES ON ISSUES IN INTERNATIONAL INVESTMENT AGREEMENTS II (2012).

UNCTAD, Expropriation: A Sequel, in UNCTAD SERIES ON ISSUES IN INTERNATIONAL INVESTMENT AGREEMENTS II (2012).

UNCTAD, Reform of Investor-State Dispute Settlement in Search of a Roadmap, Issue N. 3 (June 2013).

UNCTAD, WORLD INVESTMENT REPORT—REFORMING INTERNATIONAL INVESTMENT GOVERNANCE (2015).

Van Haersolte-Van Hof, Jacomijn J., & Hoffmann, Anne K, The Relationship Between International Tribunals and Domestic Courts, in THE OXFORD HANDBOOK ON INTERNATIONAL INVESTMENT LAW (Peter Muchlinski, Federico Ortino, & Christoph Schreuer eds., 2008).

Vandevelde, Kenneth J., The Bilateral Investment Treaty Program of the United States, 21 CORNELL INT'L L.J. 201 (1988).

Vandevelde, Kenneth J. Reassessing the Hickenlooper Amendment, 29 VA. J. INT'L L. 115 (1988).

Vandevelde, Kenneth J., The Political Economy of a Bilateral Investment Treaty, 92 AM. J. INT'L L. 621 (1998).

VATTEL, E. THE LAW OF NATIONS, OR THE PRINCIPLES OF NATURAL LAW (Béla Kapossy & Richard Whatmore eds. 2008.

Veeder, V.V., The Lena Goldfields Arbitration: The Historical Roots Of Three Ideas, 47 INT'L & COMP. L.Q. 718 (1998).

Vesel, Scott, Clearing A Path Through A Tangled Jurisprudence: Most-Favored-Nation Clauses and Dispute Settlement Provisions in Bilateral Investment Treaties, *32* YALE J. INT'L L. 125 (2007).

Waibel *et al. (eds)*, The Backlash against Investment Arbitration: Perceptions and Reality (Kluwer Law, 2010).

Wälde, Thomas, Investment Arbitration as a Discipline for Good Governance: Overview and Epilogue, [Oil, Gas & Energy Law], issue 2, 2004.

Wälde, Thomas 'The "Umbrella" Clause in Investment Arbitration: A Comment on Original Intentions and Recent Cases', 6 J. World Investment & Trade 183 (2005).

Walker Jr., Herman, Modern Treaties of Friendship, Commerce and Navigation, 42 MINN. L. REV. 805 (1958).

Wallace Jr., Don, Case Study under NAFTA: Lessons for the Wise?, in ARBITRATING FOREIGN INVESTMENT DISPUTES: PROCEDURAL AND SUBSTANTIVE LEGAL ASPECTS (Stefan Michael Kroll and Norbert Horn eds. Kluwer Law International 2004).

Wallace, Jr., Don, Fair and Equitable Treatment and Denial of Justice: Loewen v US and Chattin v Mexico, in INTERNATIONAL LAW AND ARBITRATION: LEADING CASES FROM THE ICSID, NAFTA, BILATERAL TREATIES AND CUSTOMARY INTERNATIONAL LAW (Todd Weiler ed., 2005).

WEILER, TODD, INTERPRETATION OF INTERNATIONAL INVESTMENT LAW (Martinus Nijhoff, 2013).

WILSON, ROBERT R., UNITED STATES COMMERCIAL TREATIES AND INTERNATIONAL LAW (New Orleans: The Hauser Press, 1960).

Wong, Jarrod, Umbrella Clauses in Bilateral Investment Treaties: Of Breaches of Contract, Treaty Violations, and the Divide Between Developing and Developed Countries in Foreign Investment Disputes, Geo. Mason L. Rev. 135 (2006).

Yackee, Jason W., Bilateral Investment Treaties, Credible Commitment, and the Rule of (International) Law: Do BITs Promote Foreign Direct Investment?, 42 Law & Society Review 805 (2008).

Table of Arbitration Cases

Abal Hermanos S.A. v. Uruguay, ICSID Case No. ARB/10/7, Decision on Jurisdiction (July 2, 2013).

AES Summit Generation Limited and AES-Tisza Erömü Kft v. The Republic of Hungary, ICSID Case No. ARB/07/22, IIC 455 (2010), Award (17 September, 2010).

Alasdair Ross Anderson and Others v Costa Rica, ICSID Case No ARB(AF)/07/3, IIC 437, Award (May 10th, 2010).

Americas, Inc. v. The United Mexican States, ICSID Case No. ARB (AF)/04/5 (Rovine Separate Opinion, 20 September 2007).

Antoine Goetz and others v Republic of Burundi, ICSID Case No ARB/01/2, Award, (June 21, 2012).

Aramco v. Saudi Arabia (1963) 27 I.L.R. 117.

Asian Agricultural Products Ltd. (AAPL) v. Republic of Sri Lanka. Case No. ARB/87/3, 30 ILM 577 (1991).

Bayindir Insaat Turizm Ticaret Ve Sanayi A.S. v. Islamic Republic of Pakistan, ICSID Case No. ARB/03/29, IIC 27 (2005), Decision on Jurisdiction, (November 14th, 2005).

BP Exploration Co (Libya) Ltd. v. Government of the Libyan Arab Republic, 53 ILR 297 (October 10, 1973).

Burlington Resources Inc. v. Republic of Ecuador, ICSID Case No. ARB/08/5, Decision on the Proposal for Disqualification of Professor Francisco Orrego Vicuña (13 De. 2013).

Burlington Resources Inc. v. Republic of Ecuador, ICSID Case No. ARB/08/5, Decision on Ecuador's Counterclaims (February 7th, 2017).

CME Czech Republic B.V. v. The Czech Republic, Ad hoc Tribunal (UNCITRAL) Final award and separate opinion, (March 14th, 2003).

Government of the State of Kuwait v. The American Independent Oil Company (AMINOIL) 21 ILM 976 (March 24, 1982).

Inceysa Vallisoletane, SL v El Salvador, Award, ICSID Case No ARB/03/26, IIC 134, Award, (August 2, 2006).

Inmaris Perestroika Sailing Maritime Services GmbH and others v Ukraine, ICSID Case No. ARB/08/8, Award (Mar. 1, 2012).

Lauder v. Czech Republic, 9 ICSID Rep. 62 (2001).

Libyan American Oil Company v Libyan Arab Republic, 62 ILR 140 (April 12, 1977).

Loewen Group, Inc. v. United States of America, ICSID Case No. ARB(AF)/98/3, Award (June 26, 2003).

Maffezini v. Spain, ICSID Case No. ARB/97/7 (Jan. 25, 2000), 5 ICSID Rep. 396 (2002).

Methanex Corporation v. United States of America, UNCITRAL Award (August 3rd, 2005).

Malaysian Historical Salvors v. Malaysia, ICSID Case No. ARB/05/10, Decision on Application for Annulment (Apr. 16, 2009).

MTD Equity Sdn. Bhd. and MTD Chile S.A. v. Republic of Chile, ICSID Case No. ARB/01/7, IIC 174, Award (May 25th, 2004).

Neer v. United Mexican States, 4 R. Int'l Arb. Awards 60 (Mex-U.S. Cl. Comm'n Oct. 15, 1926).

Occidental Petroleum Corp and Occidental Exploration and Production Company v Republic of Ecuador, ICSID Case No. ARB/06/11, Award, (Oct. 5th, 2012).

Perenco Ecuador Ltd. v. The Republic of Ecuador and Empresa Estatal Petróleos del Ecuador (Petroecuador), ICSID Case No. ARB/08/6, Interim Decision on the Environmental Counterclaim (August 11, 2015).

Petroleum Development (Trucial Coast) Ltd. v. Sheikh of Abu Dhabi (1951) 18 I.L.R. 144, (1951) 18 I. L. R. 144.

Philip Morris Brands Sàrl, Philip Morris Products S.A. and Abal Hermanos S.A. v. Oriental Republic of Uruguay, ICSID Case No. ARB/10/7 (2016).

Phoenix Action, Ltd. v. The Czech Republic, ICSID Case No. ARB/06/5 (April 15th, 2009).

Plama Consortium Limited v. Republic of Bulgaria, ICSID Case No. ARB/03/24, IIC 338, Award (August 27th, 2008).

Romak S.A. (Switzerland) *v.* The Republic of *Uzbekistan*, UNCITRAL, PCA Case No. AA280 (2009).

Ruler of Qatar v. International Marine Oil. Co. Ltd, (1953) 20. ILR 534.

Salini Costruttori S.P.A. v. Morocco, ICSID Case No. ARB/00/4, Decision on Jurisdiction (July 23, 2001), 42 I.L.M. 609 (2003).

Société Général de Surveillance S.A. v. Pakistan, ICSID Case No. ARB/01/13, Objections to Jurisdiction, (Aug. 5, 2003), 18 ICSID Rev. 301 (2003).

Société Général de Surveillance S.A. v. Philippines, ICSID Case No. ARB/02/6, Objections to Jurisdiction, 136–55 (Jan. 29, 2004), 8 ICSID Rep. 518 (2005).

Texaco Overseas Petroleum Company and California Asiatic Oil Company v Government of Libya, (Preliminary Award), 53 ILR 389 (Nov. 27, 1975).

Tidewater Inc., Tidewater Investment SRL, Tidewater Caribe, *C.A., et al.* v. The Bolivarian Republic of Venezuela, ICSID Case No. ARB/10/5, Decision on Claimants' Proposal to Disqualify Professor Brigitte Stern, Arbitrator (23 Dec. 2010).

Venezuela Holdings v. Venezuela, ICSID Case No. ARB/07/27, Decision on jurisdiction (June 10, 2010).

World Duty Free Company Limited v. Republic of Kenya, ICSID Case No. ARB/00/7, Award (October 2006).

Yukos Universal Limited (Isle of Man) v. The Russian Federation, UNCITRAL, PCA Case N. AA 227, Final Award (July 18th 2014).

Other Cases

Anglo-Iranian Oil Co. (U.K. v. Iran), 1952 I.C.J. 93 (July 22).

Barcelona Traction Light and Power (Belg. v. Spain) 1964 I.C.J. 6 (July 24).

Case Concerning The Factory at Chorzow, 1928 P.C.J.I. (ser. A) No. 17 (Sept. 13).

Elettronica Sicula S.p.A. (ELSI) (U.S. v. It.), 1989 I.C.J. 15 (July 20).

Factory at Chorzów, Judgment 1928 P.C.I.J. (ser. A) No. 17 p. 47. (Sept. 13).

The Mavrommatis Palestine Concessions, 1924 P.C.J.I. (ser. A) No. 2 (Aug. 30).

Table of Treaties

Agreement between the Government of the Republic of Costa Rica and the Government of Canada for the Protection and Promotion of Investment (18 March 1998), entered into force 29 September 1999 (Costa Rica-Canada BIT).

Agreement between the Federal Republic of Germany and the Republic of the Philippines on the Promotion and Reciprocal Protection of Investments (April 18, 1997) entered into force 29 September 1999 (Germany-Philippines BIT).

Agreement Between the Government of Japan and the Government of the Russian Federation Concerning the Promotion and Protection of Investment, Japan-Russ., Nov. 13, 1998.

Agreement for the Reciprocal Protection of Investments signed between the Republic of El Salvador and the Kingdom of Spain, (14 February 1995) 1983 UNTS 349, entered into force 20 February 1996.

Bilateral Investment Treaty between the Government of India and the Government of [Country] Model BIT.

Convention on the Settlement of Investment Disputes between States and Nationals of Other States *adopted* Mar. 18, 1965, 575 U.N.T.S. 159.

Havana Charter for an International Trade Organization, U.N. Doc. E/Conf. 2/78, at 14 (Mar. 24, 1948).

North American Free Trade Agreement, Dec. 8–Dec. 17, 1993, 32 I.L.M. 289 (1993).

OECD Draft Convention on Protection of Foreign Property, 7 I.L.M. 117 (1967).

The Common Market for Eastern and Southern Africa (COMESA) Investment Agreement (2007).

The Comprehensive Economic and Trade Agreement, between Canada, the European Union and its Member States, EUROPEAN COMM'N, CONSOLIDATED CETA TEXT (2014).

Energy Charter Treaty, 2080 UNTS 95 (1994).

EU—Vietnam Free Trade Agreement (Open for signature Dec. 2 2015, not yet in effect).

EU—Mexico Free Trade Agreement (updated text as of April 2017, not in effect).

France-Ecuador Bilateral Investment Treaty (1994).

Southern African Development Community (SADC) Model BIT (July 2012).

Trans-Pacific Partnership (TPP) Agreement (Opened for signature February 4 2016, not yet in effect).

Transatlantic Trade and Investment Partnership: Trade in Services, Investment and E Commerce 17, European Commission Draft Text TTIP (updated as of 2015).

Treaty of Amity, Commerce, and Navigation, Between His Britannic Majesty and the United States of America (Jay Treaty), US-U.K., Nov. 19, 1794, 8 Stat. 116, T.S. 105, 12 Bevans 13.

Treaty of Friendship, Commerce and Navigation, Nov. 28, 1956, U.S.-S. Kor., art. XXIV, 8 U.S.T. 2217, T.I.A.S. No. 3947.

Treaty of Friendship, Establishment and Navigation, Feb. 23, 1962, U.S.-Lu., art. XVII, 14 U.S.T. 251, T.I.A.S. No. 5306.

Treaty of Friendship, Commerce and Navigation, Aug. 23, 1951, U.S.-Isr., art. XXIV, 5 U.S.T. 550, T.I.A.S. No. 2948.

Treaty between the Government of the United States of America and the Government of [Country] Concerning the Encouragement and Reciprocal Protection Investment [US Model BIT 2012].

U.S.-*Colombia* Trade Promotion Agreement, U.S.-Colom., Nov. 22, 2006.

U.S.-Peru Trade Promotion Agreement, U.S.-Peru, April 12, 2006.

U.N. Material

Charter of Economic Rights and Duties of States, G.A. Res. 3281 (XXIX), U.N. Doc. A/9631 (Dec. 12, 1974).

Declaration on the Establishment of a New International Economic Order, G.A. Res. 3201 (S-VI), U.N. Doc. A/RES/S-6/3201 (May 1, 1974).

Draft Articles on Responsibility of States for Internationally Wrongful Acts, in Report of the International Law Commission on the Work of Its Fifty-third Session, UN GAOR, 56th Sess., Supp. No. 10, at 43, UN Doc. A/56/10 (2001).

UNCITRAL Arbitration Rules, G.A. Res. 65/22, UN Doc. A/RES/65/22 (2010).

U.N. Secretary-General, The Promotion of the International Flow of Private Capital, U.N. Doc. E/3325 (1960).

Visited Websites

ENCYCLOPÆDIA BRITANNICA, http://www.britannica.com/event/Don-Pacifico-affair

European Commission website, https://ec.europa.eu/

Global Affairs Canada, NAFTA Free Trade Commission, http://www.international.gc.ca/

ICSID website, https://icsid.worldbank.org/

INVESTMENT POLICY HUB, http://investmentpolicyhub.unctad.org/IIA/AdvancedSearchBITResults

Office of the United States Trade Representatives (USTR): Summary of Objectives for the NAFTA Renegotiation, https://ustr.gov/sites/default/files/files/Press/Releases/NAFTAObjectives.pdf

Regional Comprehensive Economic Partnership (RCEP), http://asean.org/

Trade in Services Agreement (TiSA), https://ustr.gov/TiSA

THE GROUP OF 77, http://www.g77.org/doc/

THE NEW YORK TIMES, https://www.nytimes.com

THE WASHINGTON POST, https://www.washingtonpost.com

United Nations Audiovisual Library of International Law, http://legal.un.org/avl/ha/adp/adp.html

U.S. Department of Commerce, https://www.commerce.gov